SO-BEP-593

Women, Work and Islamism

Maryam Poya is a visiting fellow at the Department of Development Studies at the Open University and a visiting lecturer at Birkbeck College and SOAS, London University.

Women, Work and Islamism

Ideology and Resistance in Iran

MARYAM POYA

ZED BOOKS
London & New York

Women, Work and Islamism was first published by
Zed Books Ltd, 7 Cynthia Street, London N1 9JF, UK,
and Room 400, 175 Fifth Avenue, New York, NY 10010, USA in 1999

Distributed in the USA exclusively by St Martin's Press, Inc.,
175 Fifth Avenue, New York, NY 10010, USA

Typeset in Joanna by Lucy Morton & Robin Gable, Grosmont
Cover designed by Andrew Corbett
Printed and bound in the United Kingdom
by Redwood Books, Trowbridge

A catalogue record for this book is available from the British Library

Library of Congress Cataloging-in-Publication Data
applied for

ISBN 1 85649 681 3 (Hb)
ISBN 1 85649 682 1 (Pb)

Contents

Acknowledgements

This book is dedicated to my children Tara, Farhad and Lily in gratitude for their love and support.

My general thanks should go first to the department of Development Studies at the Open University, where I have spent most of my academic life and from whom I received financial help towards my field research in Iran. I have been greatly helped and encouraged by David Wield and Hazel Johnson. My special thanks are to Margaret Kiloh and Janet Bujra for their tremendous intellectual and practical support. I am also indebted to Ruth Pearson and Nira Yuval-Davis for their valuable academic guidance and intellectual stimulation which shaped the skeleton of this research, and to Louise Murray and Ali Rahnema for encouraging and helping me to turn this research into a book. I owe special thanks to John Rose for reading this long text and making challenging comments and valuable corrections. Finally my thanks to my family and friends, especially Roya and Darioush, for their support and assistance during the field research in Iran.

Glossary

In this book the transliteration of Farsi (Persian) words does not use diacritical marks. These words are translated in the text when they appear for the first time; thereafter the reader may need to consult the Glossary. There are discrepancies in translation, partly because I have tried to follow what has become customary in the literature and partly because I have attempted to preserve the Farsi pronounciation of Farsi words in relation to Arabic pronunciation. This has resulted in differences of spelling: I have given both Farsi and Arabic spellings here.

Aghaye biroon   The master of the outside of the house.

Bazaar   Market-place.

Bazaari bazaar   Trader.

Chador   Literally means a tent. It is a full-length loose cover worn by women, which envelops the body from head to toe. It is normally held in place by a hand under the chin or, if the woman is very strict, under the eyes. At official gatherings women usually wear a black *chador*, while on unofficial occasions women might choose to wear a colourful *chador*.

Chadori   Women who wear the *chador*.

Dooreh   Getting together socially on a regular basis.

Eddeh (*Idda*)   A period of celibacy immediately after divorce or the death of a husband, during which the woman may not remarry. This is normally for three menstrual cycles, and its purpose is to determine whether the woman is bearing a child from her previous husband.

Enghelabe Farhangi Eslami   Islamic Cultural Revolution.

Farsi The official and predominant language in Iran.

Fesad Moral degeneration.

Ghalibaf Carpet weaver.

Gharbzadegi Westoxication; being influenced by western culture. The term is used to describe those Iranians who embrace western culture without reservation. *Gharbzadeh* is the person who is Westoxicated.

Ghesas (Qisas) Retribution for killing or injuring. The law of *Ghesas* is the penal law of the Islamic Republic and is based on the idea of the victim or victim's family having the right to retribution against the perpetrator of a crime against them.

Hadith The collected record of sayings and actions of the Prophet and Shii Imams. The importance of Hadith is second to that of Quran as the basis of Islamic jurisprudence.

Hejab (Hijab) Literally means a partition or curtain. It describes a type of women's clothing which protects her body from the eyes of men who are forbidden to her. Women who did not fully observe the *hejab* were called *bad hejabi*.

Hezbollahi Partisan of God. Fanatical supporters of Ayatollah Khomeini described themselves as *Hezbollahis*, conveying the meaning that they do not belong to earthly political parties and only follow God's word by following their leader Ayatollah Khomeini.

Jahad (Jihad) Islamic holy war against infidels, or to spread Islam. It is a duty of every Muslim man to participate in *jahad* if called upon. Women can play a role in a defensive *jahad* but not in an offensive one. Its current usage in the Islamic Republic also refers to the endeavour and sacrifices of the people for various Islamic and national causes.

Jahizieh Trousseau.

Jangali Forest people.

Karfarma Employer.

Kargahe Khanegi Household workshop.

Kargar Low-status workers.

Karmand Middle- to high-status workers.

Khaharane Zaynab Zaynab Sisters.

Khanome khaneh The lady of the house.

Konkour   A highly competitive examination system to enter universities and higher educational institutions.

Maghnaeh   A large scarf covering head, hair and shoulders. It has been worn with *roposh* as the dominant form of *hejab* in Iran since 1981.

Mahr   Bride-price agreed between the families of the bride and groom and written into the marriage contract. It is supposed to be paid by the husband to the wife on demand after consummation of the marriage. But the normal practice is for it to be paid on divorce.

Majles (Majlis)   The Iranian national assembly or parliament.

Majles Khebregan   The Assembly of Experts.

Mujahedeen   Warrior for God.

Nafagheh   Maintenance or alimony. In Shii Iran a husband is responsible, during the whole period of marriage, for the maintenance and upkeep of his wife and children. *Nafaghe* is also payable after divorce by a man to a woman if she has custody of the children.

Namahram   Men or women who are forbidden to each other.

Ojratolmesl   According to the reformed divorce law, if a man decides to divorce his wife unjustly he has to pay compensation to her, the equivalent of her contribution to the family throughout the years that they lived together.

Olama   Islamic religious scholars.

Rejal   Statesmen.

Roposh   A long, loose dress with long sleeves, the dominant form of *hejab* in Iran since 1981.

SAVAK   The Secret Police under the Pahlavi.

Shamsi   Solar.

Sharia   Islamic canonical law. Refers to the totality of Islamic rules, encompassing all affairs of the Muslim community.

Shii (Shiism)   A branch of Islam whose founders were partisans and followers of Ali, the Prophet's son-in-law. *Shii* believe that after the Prophet's death the leadership of Islam should have gone to Ali.

Shora   Workers' councils during the 1979 revolution.

Shoraye Negahban   The Council of Guardians, established in 1980 as a constitutional body in charge of reviewing or vetoing on religious grounds Parliamentary Bills.

Sigheh (Muta)   Used as both noun and verb for temporary marriage. It is a practice that is confined to the Shii branch of Islam, in which every man is entitled to have as many *sigheh* wives as he wishes. It is a form of marriage based on a contract, which is bound by a time-limit of between one hour and ninety-nine years. Its aim is satisfaction of sexual urges, but children born in *sigheh* marriages are legitimate.

Tabaghe   Social status.

Tisab   Acid.

Velayat Fagih   The guardianship of Islamic jurisprudence. It refers to Ayatollah Khomeini's thesis about the guardianship of the *fagih* high-ranking cleric lying with the head of state, which constitutes the basis of the Constitution of the Islamic Republic.

Zaifeh   Literally means the weak half, a derogatory term used for women.

Zakat   Islamic tax.

Zena (Zina)   Fornication, adultery, sexual intercourse between men and women who are not married to each other. In the Islamic Republic *Zena* is a crime punishable by flogging or stoning to death.

Chronology

Dates of publication of sources in Farsi (the official and predominant language in Iran) are according to the Iranian calendar. The Iranian *Shamsi* (solar) calendar year starts on 21 March. An Iranian year may be converted to the international year by adding 621. For example, the Iranian year 1343 refers to the period between 21 March 1964 and 20 March 1965, and will appear in the text as 1964/5. Throughout the book I have used this system of conversion for all Farsi sources where the date of publication is according to the Iranian calendar.

1890–92   Protest against tobacco concession given to Britain. Women played an important role in cancelling the concession.

1905–11   Constitutional revolution establishes a Constitution and a parliament *Majles*. Formation of diverse women's movements, resulting in the establishment of girls' schools in 1907.

1917–25   Women's participation in nationalist and communist movements.

1925   Reza Khan becomes Shah, beginning the Pahlavi dynasty.

1935–36   Reza Shah initiates campaign to force women to abandon the veil in all public places.

1938   Women are admitted to Tehran University.

1941   Allied forces occupy Iran, forcing Reza Shah's abdication in favour of his son Mohammad Reza Shah.

1951   Mossadegh becomes prime minister of Iran. Nationalisation of oil. Rise of women's movements within nationalist and communist movements.

1953   Mossadegh is overthrown in a CIA-backed coup.

1957	Shah's secret service, SAVAK, is created with the help of the CIA.
1958	State control over women's movements. Various women's organisations are grouped into a High Council of Women. Ashraf Pahlavi, the Shah's twin sister, heads the new organisation.
1963	Shah declares his 'White Revolution'. Uprising against the Shah, violent demonstrations in major cities. Women achieve electoral rights.
1964	Ayatollah Khomeini sent into exile; he goes first to Turkey then to Iraq.
1966	State control over women's movements. The Women's Organisation of Iran is established.
1967	Majles passes Family Protection Laws. Women are accepted into the judiciary and drafted into the police and the army.
1971	Price of crude oil increases.
	Fedayeen and Mujahedeen guerrilla organisations are established.
1973	In Tehran the Gulf states agree to double the price of oil to $11.65 a barrel.
1977	**May** A group of leading intellectuals protests against the Shah.
	June Protest of shanty-town dwellers against slum clearances.
1978	Formation of women's organisations.
	January Shah attacks Ayatollah Khomeini in the media. Theology students riot in Qom.
	February Mass demonstrations in Tabriz.
	March Spread of mass demonstrations to other urban areas.
	August First wave of industrial strikes.
	September Ayatollah Khomeini calls for the overthrow of the Shah. Martial law is declared in Tehran and eleven other cities. Black Friday: hundreds of protesters are killed by police in Tehran. Telecommunications and other workers go on strike.
	October Ayatollah Khomeini is forced to leave Iraq and goes to Paris. Oil workers go on strike.
	November Shah appoints military government. National Television employees go on strike. Bank workers go on strike. Ayatollah Khomeini calls for Islamic Republic.
	December Millions protest on the streets against the Shah. General strike brings the economy to a halt.

1979   **January** Shah flees the country.

February Ayatollah Khomeini returns to Iran and forms the Provisional Revolutionary Government. Armed insurrection. The Shah's Imperial Guard is defeated by revolutionaries. Army declares its neutrality. Political prisoners are released. Ayatollah Khomeini suspends Family Protection Laws. Formation of workers' *shoras*.

March Appointment of women as judges is stopped. Women are dismissed from military service. Ayatollah Khomeini announces that women must wear Islamic dress. Thousands of women demonstrate against the imposition. Segregation of sports and education is proposed.

April Women lawyers demand the installation of women judges. A referendum decides Iran is to be an Islamic Republic.

May Co-education is banned. Creation of Revolutionary Guards.

June Married women are banned from attending high schools. The swearing-in ceremony of new judges takes place without the participation of women nominees. Women occupy Ministry of Justice for five days. Women employees of the Communication Corporation protest against the closure of the day-care centre at their workplace. They are threatened with mass lay-off. This is the first incident in the subsequent series of nursery closures.

July Many women are flogged in public on charges of swimming in the men's section of the Caspian Sea. Three women are executed on charges of prostitution and corruption.

August Government cracks down on the left, Kurds and other ethnic minorities.

September Ayatollah Khomeini declares *Velayat faqih*. The Assembly of Experts approves the divine authority of the *faqih* over state and society. At the School of Divinity in Mashhad University segregated classes are instituted.

October New family legislation is ratified by the Council of Revolution giving right to divorce, *sighe* and the custody of children exclusively to men. Women's demonstrations against the new legislation is attacked by *Hezbollah*.

November Women occupy Ministry of Justice against the new family law. Tehran's prostitute quarter is closed. Over fifty hostages are taken from the US embassy. The conference of Women's Solidarity Council is held by candlelight, as the electricity supply of Tehran Polytechnic was cut off by the authorities in an attempt to stop the conference.

December The Islamic Constitution is ratified.

1980   **February** Wearing of Islamic dress is made compulsory for nurses and other women employees of the Ministry of Health.

March Four women are elected to the new *Majles*.

April USA imposes economic sanctions. Closure of the universities for 'Islamic Cultural Revolution'.

May Fatimah's birthday (daughter of the Prophet Mohammad) is declared as Women's Day in Iran. Women not complying with Islamic dress are attacked and knifed in urban areas; shops refuse to sell goods to them.

June Ayatollah Khomeini decrees that women are required to wear Islamic dress.

July Implementation of compulsory Islamic dress starts. Women who do not comply are dismissed from their jobs. Women's demonstrations are attacked by *Hezbollah*.

September The beginning of the Iran–Iraq war.

1981   All political organisations, women's organisations and workers' organisations are banned and cease to exist.

July The Bill of Retribution is ratified.

November Maryam Behrouzi, a delegate of the *Majles*, attends the Population Conference in China and declares that abortion and sterilisation are against Islamic rules.

1982   The government presents a draft bill on women's part-time work to the *Majles*.

1984   *Zane Rouz* women's magazine criticises state policy on polygamy for being lax on men and unjust to women. Three of the women *Majles* deputies are re-elected. Women's entry to a range of technical, engineering and experimental sciences is prohibited.

1985   *Zane Rouz* continues to discuss the problems of unclear law, uncoordinated court verdicts and the unsatisfactory treatment of women by the courts.

January The High Council of Judiciary announces that a special civil appeal court has been set up to look into family disputes not satisfactorily resolved by the *Sharia* courts. This signifies the failure of the system and women's growing protest against the system.

1986   Iran continues to export one million barrels of oil per day despite the war. Reagan admits arms sales to Iran. OPEC cuts production to increase price of oil, which reaches US$13 a barrel.

1987   OPEC agrees to increase production by 5 per cent and maintain price at US$18 a barrel.

1988   Iran accepts UN Security Resolution 598, for immediate ceasefire. The state initiates a public debate about population control and the dangers of uncontrolled population growth. The three existing women *Majles* deputies are re-elected.

1989   Women's magazines discuss methods of birth control extensively and recommend a wide variety of contraception. An authoritative collection of the Islamic Republic's family laws brought together a number of sources of guidance on the family, including the Civil Code of 1931, the Family Protection Law of 1967 and 1975, the Special Civil Courts Act 1979, other legislations passed by the *Majles* and the various decrees of Ayatollah Khomeini.

        May The policy on women's entry to higher education becomes less restrictive. It is announced that restrictions on women's entry to geology and agriculture are lifted.

        June Ayatollah Khomeini dies; Hashemi Rafsanjani is elected President.

        July The Ministry of Health announces the government's policy on population control, based on distribution of free contraceptives through health centres in rural and urban areas, covering 90 per cent of the population.

1990   President Rafsanjani defends his policy of encouraging foreign investment.

        Ayatollah Sanei expresses strong Islamic opposition to polygamy and raises the question of the acceptability of abortion as a method of birth control.

1992   The Office of Women's Affairs is created. Nine women are elected to the *Majles*.

        November–December *Zanan* women's magazine is published for the first time and publishes a series of articles challenging the established view that women cannot become judges.

1993   **Autumn** *Farzaneh* women's magazine is published for the first time, containing a series of articles on women's high position in Islam.

1995   **September** A large number of delegates attend Beijing Conference on Women.

1996   **January** The Ministry of Justice appoints 200 women judicial counsellors to preserve women's rights in courts more satisfactorily.

March–April In the *Majles* election 190 women candidates campaign for changes in the law, and better education and employment legislation for women. Thirteen women are elected.

October The *Majles* approves a motion presented by women deputies to create the Special Commission on Women's and Family's Affairs to reform laws to improve the protection of women's rights.

1997   **July** Nine women stand for President as a protest against women's ineligibility. Women's magazines campaign in favour of Khatami, the pragmatic candidate, as opposed to Ayatollah Nouri, the hardline cleric. Women's votes play an important role in President Khatami's victory.

1998   *Hoghogheh Zanan* magazine is published for the first time, concentrating on the question of violence against women.

Anjomane Senfieh Rouznamenegaran Zan (Women journalists' trade association) formed.

March A women's publishers' book exhibition displays books published by 47 women's publishers. By early 1999 the number of women's publishers has increased to 236.

August *Rouznameh Zan* is published for the first time and campaigns for the inclusion of women in the Assembly of Experts. As a result of this campaign, ten women stand for this election, and are declared unqualified.

December Parvaneh Eskandari Forouhar, a well-known political activist, alongside a number of writers, poets and other activists, was murdered by conservative elements in a terrorist attack. Despite these attacks, a democracy movement is struggling for the establishment of civil society in Iran.

Chapter 1

Introduction

This book questions gender relations under Islamism in Iran through an analysis of the relationship between changes in women's employment, religious ideology and the Iranian state. Initially I wanted to explore the growth in women's employment in Iran. But in the course of my research it became apparent that this issue cannot be separated from the wider issues of the role of the state and economic and ideological factors which are historically determined and therefore changing at different periods. The contradictions arising from this complex relationship raise the issue of women's resistance and the role in it of social class. This involves an overlap between secularity and religion in the period under investigation (1980s and 1990s).

My main argument is that women's struggle for change has led to a questioning of gender relations. This in turn has challenged Islamic theology and thereby the Iranian theocratic state, with the result that the state has been forced to adapt its ideological position and practices. Whereas Islamic theology and the state treat women as a unitary category, women's responses to employment and to the state have been differentiated by their socio-economic position and level of religious observance. Women in Iran are not a homogeneous category, and so it is necessary to analyse the experiences in employment of women of different classes and with different levels of adherence to religious ideology. This makes it possible to assess the nature of women's struggle for change and the impact that this has had on state ideology and on gender relations in both the public and the private spheres.

There are two objectives in researching the specific issue of women's experiences in the labour market and the labour force: first, my personal interest in the role of women in Iran. After some years in exile, the 1979 revolution provided an opportunity for me to go back to Iran and become politically active in the revolutionary movement. My activities in the women's movement and particularly my involvement with women workers in their struggle within workers' *shoras* (councils or grassroots trade union movements), which developed in this period in Iran, inspired me and created the rationale for researching the issue of women's employment.

My second objective is to solve an academic puzzle – the inter-action between economic factors, ideological factors and women's responses. Thus, there are a number of questions that I am investigating: how women's employment, even within an Islamic framework, has undermined the Islamic state's ideology of female seclusion and its stated gender relationships; how women responded to economic forces and the ideological underpinning of the Iranian state; how the issue of women's employment is related to the role of the state, class and ideology.

This research is original in a number of ways. Women's employment has not yet been described, identified, analysed and included within Iranian women's studies. This omission is the result of giving too much attention to the importance of ideology and not taking into consideration the interaction between ideology, economy and gender. The research into women's life histories and work histories laid the groundwork for identifying research questions and locating different theoretical approaches to analysing and explaining the research questions.

My aim, therefore, is to contribute to the debate on women's issues in Iran in the hope that this will locate women at the centre of the analysis of development rather than at the periphery, and have a practical outcome in terms of showing both women and policy makers the importance of this issue.

The Iranian Revolution and the Birth of the Islamic State

In February 1979 the regime of the oppressive, modernising Pahlavi rulers of Iran (Reza Shah, 1925–41, and Mohammad Reza Shah, 1941–79) was overthrown by a popular revolution. The large-scale participation of women in the revolutionary movement raised hopes that the role of women in Iranian society would change.

The state under the Pahlavi, as the agent of economic development, created favourable conditions for the expansion of capital. But it strengthened patriarchal structures throughout society. By 'patriarchy' I mean a set of power relations which explains women's subordination to men. Women experienced the economic, political and social changes differently to men. Through women's struggles for change some reforms were achieved. These reforms, however, touched the lives of only a minority of women – those who had access to plentiful material resources. As a result, women's reaction to these changes differed according to their class and degree of religious observance. Consequently, there were at least two different groups of women in the revolutionary movements of 1978–79. Many women participated out of dissatisfaction with the reforms made under the Pahlavi system, because they did not go far enough. At the same time, there were many women who supported the revolution because they supported the Islamic leaders and their criticisms of the Pahlavi state, including their view that the role of women is distinct from that of men. These issues will be discussed in Chapter 2.

In April 1979 a referendum decided that Iran was to be an Islamic Republic under the leadership of Ayatollah Khomeini. The reinforcement of Islamic gender relations was a major feature of the ideology of the new rulers. For years prior to the 1979 revolution, prominent Shii olama (Islamic scholars) such as Khomeini (1987–88), Mottahari (1981) and Nouri (1964–65) criticised the Pahlavi reforms for promoting a capitalist and imperialist culture of consumerism, which included the selling of women's labour. They argued that these reforms resulted in fesad (moral degeneration) and the breakdown of family values. After the establishment of the Islamic state, this view became dominant among the Islamists, and authorised the clergy to preach the ideology of seclusion, the complete withdrawal of women from the public sphere of employment and their confinement to the private sphere of the home. At the heart of this position was a belief that reproduction is the basic law of nature, and that the biological differences between the sexes give biological men and women specific roles and functions. They argued strongly that women's primary activity is in the home, nurturing and creating an atmosphere of shelter and comfort for their family.

The Debate between Secular and Muslim Iranian Feminists

In the 1980s and early 1990s, two opposing arguments dominated the debate in Iran about women's position under the Islamic state. The secular feminists, mostly writing from exile (Moghadam 1994; Moghadam 1993a, 1993b; 1988; Afshar 1991, 1989, 1987, 1985, 1982; Sanasarian 1986, 1982; Azari 1983; Nashat 1983; Tabari and Yeganeh 1982), challenged the Islamic state and its laws and regulations with regard to women's position both within and outside the home, arguing that the Islamisation of the state had marginalised women's activities in the economic, social and political spheres. Inside Iran, on the other hand, Muslim feminists (Rahnavard n.d.; Hashemi 1980, 1981; Etezadi Tabatabai 1979, 1981) argued that the Islamisation of the state liberated Iranian women from being treated, as under the Pahlavi, as commodities and sex objects.

I use the term 'secular feminists' to refer to those feminists who may see religious influence in society as negative and demand an end to the hegemony of religion over civil society and the separation of religion from the state. I use the term 'Muslim feminists' to refer to those feminists who, within the Islamic framework, in a variety of ways (intellectually, politically or as activists) demand women's rights through reforms of Islamic laws and regulations (Tohidi 1996: 280).

The opposing views of secular and Muslim feminists had one common feature, in that they examined Islamic ideology and the role of religious leaders and institutions in Iran, but they arrived at different conclusions. At the centre of the secularists' argument was the view that the position of women in Iran has been deeply affected by the writings and attitudes of Shii *olama* (Khomeini 1987–88, 1979; Mottahari 1981; Majlesi 1979; Tabatabai 1979–80; Nouri 1964–65). They pointed to a number of areas – such as breadwinning in the family, Islamic family law, biological differences between the sexes, the differential process of socialisation of the sexes and the importance of the honour of the family – as evidence of the marginalisation of women in the public sphere.

Some writers (Moghadam 1988: 223–8; Nashat 1983: 37–60; Afshar 1987: 70–89, 1982: 75–90) argue that the interpretation of Quranic verses by the Iranian *olama* constitutes the rationale for putting men entirely in charge of household expenditure, and is therefore responsible for the socio-economic inequality between the genders. According to this interpretation a woman has to be protected, looked after and controlled. The man is obliged to provide food, shelter and clothing for his wife and children. In return the woman has obligations towards her husband including obeying his sexual demands. Men, as a result of their economic struggle, are given authority by Islamic ideology to manage the affairs of women and even to punish women if they do not comply with their rules. Thus women's rights to own and hold personal property and income become irrelevant, as they are not allowed to dispose of them without their husband's permission.

The same writers, with Yeganeh (1982), also argue that the olama assert strongly that biological differences determine the psychological, intellectual and legal status of women. From the moment of birth, therefore, girls and boys are raised and treated differently. This given identity constructs different gender roles within society. Child-bearing and child-rearing are the woman's uniquely important contribution to society. Thus marriage is an important institution that gives a woman the identity she deserves.

Furthermore, Afshar, Nashat and Yeganeh argue that the allocation of the sphere of the home to women, according to women's biological and intellectual differences, is given expression in Islamic family law, which clearly emphasises gendered socio-economic inequality and highlights the economic root of male superiority and male social and economic hegemony over women. For example, inheritance law specifies that a woman's inheritance share be half of the man's. The rationale for this is that the woman gets mahr (bride price) and nafaghe (maintenance) from her husband.

Moghadam (1994) points out that the Quran does not explicitly forbid women's participation in the job market. However, Quranic regulations concerning female sexuality lay the ground for various forms of legal discrimination and occupational segregation of female labour. Women are treated as a quasi-commodity, setting limits on the non-sexual aspects of their lives, including participation in the labour market.

These issues raised by secular feminists were debated, written about and published outside Iran to show the way women were marginalised by the Islamic state, both inside and outside the home.

Although these publications were banned in Iran, over the years they raised important questions about women's oppression in relation to changes since the 1979 revolution and the Islamisation of the state. They also raised questions for women in Iran who found themselves caught between the Islamic ideology advocating women's place in the home and the practical reality of having to go out to work in order to feed their families.

It was under these circumstances that the Islamists responded. In response to the secularist interrogation of Shii ideology, Muslim feminists constructed an ideal Islamic image of Muslim woman in the late twentieth century, to oppose the image bound up in the culture of capitalism and imperialism, which spread throughout society in the Pahlavi period.

Rahnavard (n.d.: 50–85), Hashemi (1980, 1981) and Etezadi Tabatabai (1979 and 1981) were the first Muslim feminists in Iran to argue that Islam is the only socio-economic and socio-political system which does not exploit and marginalise women, because it assigns the sphere of home to women without confining women to the home. In this context they argued that under both capitalist and communist systems women are exploited as cheap workers, oppressed as sex objects and robbed of their identity of femininity. Under Islam, a woman is encouraged to participate in economic activities, she gains and keeps the fruits of her labour and is free to invest or spend it in any way she wishes. Her work inside and outside the home is regarded as valuable and is confirmed by her entitlement to *nafaghe* – she can even charge her husband for nursing her own babies. At the same time she has no obligation to support other members of the family or the society.

These writers acknowledge the Quran's view that men and women are biologically, psychologically and intellectually different. They agree with male Islamic scholars that the cyclical nature of menstruation in women disturbs women's ability to testify and form judgements. Therefore, they argue, it is meaningless to demand equal rights for basically unequal beings. They stressed that the Quran has given different rights and responsibilities to the different creations of God. Thus, in their view, the Islamic laws and regulations concerning marriage, divorce, custody of children, *mahr* and *nafaghe* are justified. They endorse the Islamic constitution, which emphasises that motherhood is the primary task of women. But they argue that women are not prohibited from working outside the home, provided that it is strictly within an Islamic framework.

A comparison of these two opposing views shows that both secularist and Muslim feminists concentrate on ideological rather than material issues. The secularists emphasised the repressive nature of Islamic ideology and its effect on women's position within family, employment and the wider society.[1] The Islamists, on the other hand, respond by defending Islamic ideology as liberating women from the consumerism inherent in capitalism. Material issues such as the Iran–Iraq war and its aftermath, which affected women's participation in the labour force and their struggle to improve their status, were largely ignored.

In the 1990s, parliamentary and presidential elections in Iran showed that gender had become part of Islamic politics and that women played an important role in shaping this discourse; women managed to alter the religious understandings of women's position. This was reflected in the reforms of family law, education and employment policies in relation to women. Most importantly, these changes had been made possible by the collaboration between secular and religious women in Iran, who, despite their disagreement on the nature of the Islamic state, had a shared experience: the contradictions between religious thinking on gender roles and relations and the reality of their lives. These factors, combined with the activities of secular feminists (both inside and outside Iran) in opposing the Islamic state's position on women, made gender into a political issue that was constantly discussed and debated. All these factors raised gender consciousness in Iran and led to women's struggle for change.

As a result, a number of secular feminists had to review their position and acknowledge the changes in Iran. Studies by Afshar (1998), Kian (1997), Paidar (1997), Mir-Hosseini (1996, 1993a, 1993b), Haeri (1994) and Najmabadi (1991) indicate a shift in the position of the secular feminists. Afshar argues that the Islamisation of the state marginalised women in Iran in comparison with the period before the 1979 revolution. However, she recognises that women are fighting their corner and have demonstrated that they will not easily be defeated. Paidar's study of women and the political

process in twentieth-century Iran shows that, far from being marginal, the position of women was central to the political discourses
of Iran under the Islamic state. Kian argues that women in Iran,
through their involvement in politics, have forced the state to present
a different reading of Islam and Islamic laws which is more atten-
tive to the condition of women. Mir-Hosseini suggests that since
Islamists are in power in Iran and Islam is no longer part of oppo-
sitional discourse, a feminist re-reading of the Islamic position on
gender has been made possible, because Islamist women have to
deal with the contradictions of the Shii. Evidently, women in Iran
used the institution of *mahr* to negotiate a better bargaining position
in marriage and divorce. Haeri argues that many Islamist women in
Iran have used the institution of temporary marriage as a way to
escape their marginal, restricted and unfavourable status. Najmabadi
argues that women in Iran, despite strict moral codes of behaviour
imposed by the state, have turned to feminism in order to carve out
a social space of their own.

A comparison of these writings with the studies a decade earlier
of women's issues in Iran shows that in the 1980s there was no
dialogue between Muslim and secular feminists. In the 1990s dialogue took place between Muslim and secular feminists which has
led to a change in the position of a number of secular writers.
Despite this, a specific study of women in the economic context is
largely absent from this debate. From a secular position and as a
critic of Islamic-state gender relations, I started my research with
the view that Islamic gender ideology leads to the marginalisation
of women within the workforce, in comparison with the Pahlavi
period. However, through field research I learned that in the 1980s
and 1990s economic factors led to a growth in women's employment in Iran and to many women beginning to question gender
relations. Therefore my aim is to challenge the view that gender
ideology determined women's employment in Iran. A critical analysis
of these debates in the context of women's employment also allowed
me to study the conceptual relationships between state, capital and
gender ideology. Furthermore, through the analysis of women's
resistance and the role of class in this resistance, I was able to
examine change in gender consciousness, in gender relations and in
the position of the state.

Changes in the Position of the Islamic State

To assess the state's policies towards women it is important to divide the history of the period since 1979 into three phases of Islamisation. Although there are overlaps between the periods, each exhibited distinct characteristics in terms of women's employment. These are: the revolutionary period (1979–81); the Iran–Iraq war and the war economy (1981–89); and the period of reconstruction post-war, post-Ayatollah Khomeini (after 1989).

The revolution

In the period immediately after the 1979 revolution, the principles of Islamic gender relations were implemented as the policy and practice of the Iranian state. The state adopted the policy of seclusion of women – their restriction to the private domestic domain and their complete exclusion from the public sphere. During this period, the Islamic state attempted to push women back to total dependence on men by reasserting the importance of the home and family for women, and their role in producing the ideal Islamic society free from the 'corruption' and 'moral degeneration' of the Pahlavi period. The aim of the state was, therefore, to exclude women from economic, social and political activities outside the home, which were now 'public' activities, and to confine them to bearing and rearing children, and the care, socialisation and maintenance of the family, which were 'private'. This was reflected in the constitution of the Islamic Republic, which emphasised women's priority in the home (Algar 1980). Also under the influence of the olama, and in accordance with the Quran's view that women are worth only half the value of men in legal and financial matters (Quran 1955: verse 282), and are too emotional and weak to be able to make hard decisions, women were excluded from professions such as management and the judiciary.

Women were offered voluntary redundancy, early retirement and part-time work in order to have time to fulfil their duty of motherhood. The state also implemented the policy of segregation – separate spheres for women in the public domain – as another step towards their exclusion from that domain. A set of practices was therefore established, designed to control women's participation in the public economy, ranging from Islamic dress, and separate seats and queues for men and women in all public places, to a rigid sexual segregation within the law, education and employment – a form of sexual apartheid (Poya 1992). These issues will be explored in Chapter 3.

The war

The revolutionary period was very short. The Iran–Iraq war, which started in September 1980, required some rethinking of this extreme position. Whereas the policy of seclusion adopted in the period following the 1979 revolution required the complete exclusion of women from the public sphere, the policy of segregation accepted their limited and controlled involvement.

During the Iran–Iraq war (1980–88), despite Islamic gender ideology, a number of factors forced women to go out to work to feed their families. These factors included economic necessity arising from the flight of men to the war zones, and inflation and a general level of unemployment as a result of Iran's isolation in the world market, intensified by the war and the war economy. Although there was a high level of male unemployment, unemployed men were neither trained nor willing to do 'women's jobs' such as nursing, teaching, secretarial and administrative work. Women were also absorbed into the service sector, which grew as a result of the nationalisation of banks and insurance companies after the 1979 revolution, extending state employment. The Islamic state also confiscated industries and farms owned by the Pahlavi royal family and their close associates, which further increased state employment. The number of female state employees increased in consequence.

Reconstruction

The end of the war with Iraq in 1988 and the death of Ayatollah Khomeini in 1989 ushered in a third phase in the development of the Iranian state, effectively ending the policy and practice of 'neither east nor west but Islamic republic', adopted in the previous years, although the rhetoric remained strong. Opportunities for reducing Iran's isolation in the world market were developed by a gradual open-door policy to the West. Generally the level of employment increased as a result of post-war reconstruction. But a combination of inflation and male inability and unwillingness to perform women's jobs has sustained the necessity for women's participation.

The war is also important as an event that raised ideological issues. The state used the war to promote the ideology of nationalism, which played a significant role in legitimising its hegemony. Images of Iranian Muslim women became central representations of the politics of cultural autonomy and anti-western anti-imperialism. But these ideological factors interacted with material factors and affected women's expectations and position within the family and the labour market. This sheds light on the limits of the importance of ideological factors affecting women's position in the economy and society in a situation where economic pressures make a particular impact. This research challenges the orthodox academic debate on this issue, and the assumption that either the negative or the positive aspects of Islamic ideology *determine* women's position. These issues are tackled in Chapters 4 and 5.

The Role of Ideology

In each of the three periods outlined above, the Iranian state sought different ways to reconcile the reality of economic development and women's response to employment with Islamic ideology. In the first phase (1979–81), an ideal Islamic image of Muslim womanhood was constructed on the model of the lives of women in early Islam, such as Fatimah, daughter of the prophet Mohammad, and Zaynab, his granddaughter. Their lives were celebrated for representing and symbolising motherhood and womanhood: Fatimah, the perfect mother and wife in the domestic sphere, and Zaynab, who fought alongside her brothers in the battlefields but who returned in peace time to take up her exalted responsibilities as a good wife and mother, educating the new generation of Muslim men and women (Khomeini 1987–8). This image of Zaynab allowed the Islamic state to justify women's participation in the revolutionary period, despite its stated ideology that women's place is in the home. Initially, the state exploited the mobilisation of women by claiming that it was only a transition period to a truly Islamic state. During the revolutionary period, the state benefited ideologically from mass participation of religious women wearing the *chador* (long black veil) in street demonstrations. Later, during the first years of the war with Iraq, the state and the economy materially and ideologically bene-fited from the unpaid work of a large number of women in the mosques, who communally produced food and medical aid for the soldiers. The voluntary nature of the work allowed the Islamic state to continue to use the image of Zaynab in justification. Later still, as large numbers of women obtained payment for their work out-side the home, the state continued to use this form of religious moralising to justify what should have been unjustifiable.

During the second and third phases (1981–89 and 1989–90s), when, as we have seen, factors such as inflation, male unemployment and the war economy increased women's active participation in the workforce, the state continued to use the dual images of Fatimah and Zaynab ideologically to justify the return of women to the workforce in large numbers, but it still argued that women's activities in the public sphere were justified only as a temporary phase, similar to the active role of Zaynab in war, which contrasted to her more passive stance in peace. This temporary phase has, however, been prolonged.

Throughout the 1980s and 1990s, more and more families have been relying on auxiliary or solely female earnings. The new gener-ation has been politically and educationally socialised into the notion that a woman's place is in the home, although its personal experi-ences are very different. Moreover, in the same way that women who participated in the revolutionary phase experienced the impor-tance of their contribution to the political movement, those who of necessity entered the workforce during and after the war against Iraq came to realise how important their economic contribution was to their families. This experience has raised the consciousness of women generally. As a result, the Islamic state has sought to reconcile the problem of its stated gender ideology to the reality of women's situation by introducing, alongside the Fatimah and Zaynab roles for women, the concept of segregation.

The systematic use of the images of Fatimah and Zaynab, and the process of segregation, may be seen as a retreat from the ideal of seclusion. But I will argue that segregation has been relatively success-ful as a device to reconcile the needs of the economy with that of maintaining the ideological basis on which the state depends for its support. However reluctantly, this policy and practice allowed the state to perpetuate women's employment in a way that could be accommodated within its ideology. It has also been a powerful instrument to place women in a disadvantaged position within the employment hierarchy. Women are, therefore, easily excluded from upward mobility and are concentrated in low-paid, low-status jobs.

This change in the state's position allowed me to establish a conceptual framework within which the link between the findings of the field research and the academic debate about the relationship between gender[2] and development could be analysed. Through an analysis of the sexual division of labour under the Islamic state, I was able to identify women within the labour force and the labour market as waged workers, as unpaid family workers and as petty commodity producers. In other words, the sexual division of labour for women depends on the social relations of production under which the work is performed. I will also argue that an analysis of the social relations between women and men is equally important to assess the way men and women are integrated differently into the workforce. Only through an analysis of social relations of gender was I able to account for women's subordination in work, in the home and in society as a whole. Therefore, as will be argued throughout this book, this case study of Iran demonstrates that women's employment is determined by the sexual division of labour in the social relations of production and by social relations between women and men.

However, I challenge the orthodox debate about these issues.[3] I have used these analytical concepts differently within the context of Iran in the particular period under investigation and I have arrived at a different outcome. In Chapter 3, I use the concept of sexual division of labour within the context of the Islamisation of state, economy and society to show how women were initially excluded from the labour market and the labour force, but later included as a result of the war and the change in economic circumstances. But despite women's increasing participation in the economy and society, gender social relations place women at a disadvantage within the labour market and the labour force. In Chapters 4 and 5, I use the concept of social relations between women and men in the context of gendered roles in the home and in the wider society, including employment, to show patriarchal relations.[4] But I have used patriarchal relations within the context of class relations and level of religious adherence to examine the change in the form and degree of patriarchy in the Islamic state by analysing the structure of the labour market, the wage gap between women and men, the role of the state, and the role of men and women within the family and in employment.

A critical study of the literature on capitalism and patriarchy,[5] the state, capital and patriarchy,[6] and women's resistance to and struggles against patriarchal gender relations[7] enabled me to make use of the major insights gained from these feminist theories while attending to the issue of women and employment in Iran. For example, Al-Hibri's (1981) analysis of a single system of patriarchy and capitalism in Muslim societies can be applied to Iran, as patriarchal social relations are part and parcel of the process of economic development. Within this context, as suggested by Walby (1990), I have distinguished between the form and the degree of patriarchal relationship by analysing the wage gap between men and women workers as well as the patriarchal relationship within education, employment and the law.

Chhachhi's (1991) and Moghadam's (1993b) analyses are also important in understanding the role of the state as the agent of economic development and social control. I therefore use this analysis to assess the Islamic state in Iran, which in the 1990s has been seeking further integration and incorporation into the world market. For this purpose, it has abandoned its fundamentalist slogans to a great degree. It has also reformed laws and regulations in relation to women and family, education and employment. Nevertheless, the state protects and regulates the family and male domination throughout the society by exercising control over women. This is to ensure that the increase in the number of working women does not lead to the breakdown of patriarchal control.

I argue that the Islamic state under economic pressure is committed to development within global capitalism, but under ideological pressure constantly seeks effective patriarchal domination. This has created contradiction and conflict between the genders at the level of family, state and society as women constantly find ways of rebelling against these forms of patriarchal relationships.

Women's Responses

This book also addresses women's resistance through an analysis of class and the overlap between class, secularity and religion. Chapter 6 shows that the response of women to state policy has differed according to their class and level of religious observance. Through an analysis of gender relations within the context of indigenous class formation and class structure I examine the local perceptions of middle-class and working-class women. These widely used phrases refer to different socio-economic status, but both groups of women have the same relationship to the system of social production; that is, they are dependent for their survival upon the sale of their labour power. The distinction between them lies in their different access to material resources and political power, as a result of the influence of the state and capital. Another equally important distinction is the influence of religion, cross-cutting these divisions. The resulting social division is expressed in terms of a division of labour within the family and in paid employment; in gender relationships within the family and in the wider society; in attitudes to male and female roles in fertility, sexuality and education; and in power, income, wealth and even world-view.

The fact that class and ideological differences divide women, even though there are also issues that they face together, has produced different responses to the policies of the Islamic state from two main groups of women, each of which experienced contradictions. On the one hand, religious women may accept the ideology of the Islamic state which emphasises women's place in the home, but meanwhile demand reforms and equality with men in both the home and employment – until the ideal Islamic state and society is established and there is no need for women to go out to work. On the other hand, secular women, or those who do not practise religion, also demand equality with men, and they question the nature of the Islamic state and its male-dominated gender relations. More importantly, they wish to fulfil their potential through active participation in employment and career mobility, but Islamic ideology is so strong that they have little choice other than to accept the hegemony of the state and, therefore, to compromise.

The point of this book is to argue that the specific characteristics of the Islamic state mean that the way women in Iran have entered the public sphere is different from that of women in other societies, and even in Iran prior to the Islamisation of the state. These characteristics have also determined a form of state-sponsored patriarchy, which exploits women's participation in the public arena while systematically threatening women's mobility and security through the promotion of the idea that women's place is in the home.

Women's ideas are shaped by both material and ideological factors. Women of different classes and with different levels of religious observance have different notions of what liberation is and how to achieve it. Working-class and middle-class women who are religious accept the view that Islamic gender relations liberate women from the exploitation of consumerism imposed by western capitalism. The majority of these women support the state ideology, including its gender relations, but they have found a growing conflict between holding on to Islamic ideology and their economic, social and even personal material interests.

Some middle-class women who may not be religious see the Islamic state as marginalising and oppressing women, and they therefore oppose the Islamic state, even though they have no choice other than to comply with its rules and regulations. Nevertheless, as economic necessity bites deeper, women, whatever their class and level of religious observance, press harder for reforms and equality with men. These struggles take place within the Islamic framework and rhetoric. Nevertheless, women are finding ways of raising secular issues within the Islamic framework. Different organs of the media, especially numerous women's newspapers and magazines, discuss feminism, patriarchy, gender relations and even women's position in the family, education, law and employment under the Islamic state in Iran. Interaction through the media has created a form of unity between women of different classes and belief who demand change. Within this framework, a limited degree of reform is being achieved, similar to those made in the Pahlavi period.

My aim is to stress the importance of the vast diversity of women's experiences, and the conflicts and contradictions between different approaches that question oppressive categories,[8] and the way the two forms of feminism evolved in Iran as a response to those contradictions, which enabled many women to challenge existing structures in varied ways.

Chapter 6 looks at the evidence of success in improving women's status through examining measurable material factors such as women's participation in politics, reformed laws on family, education and employment and the use of media by women. Such evidence can also be found in inquantifiable factors, affecting people's personal lives and their modes of negotiation. It can be noted, for example, in the way middle-class religious women constrained by ideology and poorer women constrained not only by ideology but also by reduced access to material resources feel about holding on to the ideology but behaving differently; and in the way secular or less devout women who are less constrained by the ideology but have more access to material resources attempt to improve their status, even though their participation in the labour force is limited by the systematically segregated labour market where female workers are temporary.

In the context of women's responses to patriarchal relationships, Kandiyoti's (1991) analysis of bargaining with patriarchy is important. I use this analysis to discuss women's diverse individual responses to patriarchal relationships at home, at work and in the wider society, using material resources and ideological constraints. I will argue that the power of Islamic ideology, leadership and institutions may have reduced women's bargaining position, but within the Islamic framework a larger number of women are exposed to gender consciousness and unfavourable gender relations and are struggling to improve their status. I therefore disagree with the view that ideological factors imposed by the Islamic state determined women's employment. I argue, on the contrary, that in the period under investigation, material factors and women's responses have been as important as, if not more important than, ideological factors.

This book's argument, based on field research in Iran, is of considerable contemporary relevance for two reasons. First, the state has the power to transform gender relations but is also constrained by its own strategic imperatives – to expand the economy, to wage war, to reward allies and to deflect internal dissent. Second, the patriarchal power of men, even when backed by state power, is never unitary. Men's interests are divided and contradictory; they

cannot unite around a policy which inhibits women from economic
participation because some men's interests will dictate the use of
patriarchal power to exploit female labour whilst the interests of
others demand female exclusion.

Thus I show that women's employment, even within an Islamic
framework, has undermined the Islamic state's ideology of female
seclusion and its gender relationships. This is as a result of women's
organised and individual responses to economic forces and the
ideological underpinning of the Iranian state. This task required field
research in Iran, where there were many areas to be explored and
questions to answer.

Field Research

Gathering evidence in Iran between 1989 and 1992 was problematic.
The study of feminist debates on qualitative and quantitative methods
of analysis helped me to identify the appropriate method to gather
evidence for this book.[9] Therefore, within the context of my research questions I used a combination of qualitative methods[10]
derived from different disciplines: sociology, anthropology and oral
history. By using questionnaires and statistics I also accumulated
some quantitative data to test the validity of an explanation.[11]

The research data, therefore, includes primary sources: eighty
interviews between 1989 and 1992 with women of various occupations, and a group interview with eight men and women in 1996,
at the time of the parliamentary elections. Five hundred questionnaires were distributed in 1990 and collected in 1991 and 1992.
General observation was carried out at different stages between 1989
and 1996. The research data also includes secondary material, such
as volumes of official statistics, press reports, legislation, and published and unpublished research on women in Iran in general, as
well as specific data about women and employment in Iran.

Interviews are my most important research materials. I found a
case study of oral history methodology (Thompson 1988) useful to
explain the conflicts and struggles which my interviewees faced in
employment. This method is open to the criticism that it is too
subjectivist, biased and does not permit generalisation, which is
important for policy formation (Jayaratne 1983: 156–7). I have used

this method, however, because the validity of the evidence or aspects of it can be checked with the documentary evidence (Bornet 1992). Also, interviews with a relatively small sample of women can be qualitative, systematic and aimed at theory development. Equally important, this form of analysis allows an analysis of women as fully historical persons who struggle to improve their status. This approach is, therefore, scientific and in women's interests, for it uses precise notions, theories and processes whose results will return to women and to society (Chanfrault-Duchet 1991: 90; Jayaratne and Stewart 1991: 93).

As an active participant I was listening to my interviewees while also attending to my own response and trying to learn more from each woman. Each work history taught me a new dimension of women and work (Anderson and Jack 1991: 19). I scrutinised the meaning of different issues which emerged from each interview and I tried to understand and compare the experiences of each woman with another who was socially differentiated.

Using this method, learnt from oral historians, I was able to identify statistical information that is biased against women. For example, my interviews show that official statistics do not include categories of women workers who effectively contribute to their families' and to the national and international economy. These are unpaid agricultural workers and carpet-weavers, petty commodity producers, and a large number of women workers who are employed by many medium or small private enterprises, whose employers do not declare them as their workforce, in order to evade paying tax and insurance.

Throughout the field research my observation confirmed the validity of the interviews about women's unrecorded contributions. In the two villages that I visited in the North and the East of Iran, all women agricultural workers and carpet-weavers were unpaid family workers. Those whom I interviewed said that they had never been asked by officials whether they work or not; the officials who visit villages ask men, as heads of households, about members' economic activities. Interviewees also said that women's contribution is considered (by men and women) as natural and part of domestic life, rather than belonging to a particular category such as agricultural work or carpet-weaving. Many women workers, therefore, do not appear in the official statistics, even as unpaid workers.

My observation also confirmed the findings of my interview with ten petty commodity producers and traders: that a large number of women are engaged in this occupation. The queues of women outside the stores and shops which sell ration-coupon goods are much longer than the queues of men. These women make a living by buying cheaply from the rationing system and selling expensively on the black market. Many of my interviewees who worked for medium or small private enterprises told me that none of them was registered as a worker. This was confirmed by my observation in 1992, when I counted 150 shops in one street in northern Tehran selling female clothes. They all employed female shop assistants; on average, each shop employed three women at different times of the day, and none of them was registered as a worker.

Thus, the oral evidence and my observation led me to find out, first, that despite the official statistics which show that a large number of women work for the state, a much larger number of women work for small private enterprises. Second, this is despite the pressure of ideology, which makes seeking employment in state enterprises desirable for women and men. Third, women are working in a variety of ways in unpaid and paid employment to generate income or save expenditure for their families and increase their standard of living. Haggis (1990) argues that the choice of research method contributes to the exclusion or inclusion of women in the statistical picture, or, in other words, to the production of a feminist knowledge. More importantly, as Pugh (1990) suggests on the basis of this feminist principle, I recognised the central role of the researcher, and sought to use that positively in the research process.

The oral accounts also revealed the difference between women's and men's earnings. It is a matter of labour law that the head of a household and the breadwinner receives higher wages, in terms of benefits. But it does not make explicit that only a male person is considered as the breadwinner. It also does not record how women lose benefits because of their familial responsibilities and the absence of child-care. Some of these issues are revealed through the media and official documents. But they do not reveal the difference between women's contribution to the family in comparison to that of their husbands, nor the unequal relationship between men and women in the family and in society as a whole.

More importantly, official channels do not reveal whether access to paid employment is empowering for women. For this reason I have used four variables – the number of children, education, male financial control and women's power of decision making – to assess change in gender relationship as a result of material and ideological constraints. My calculation derives from women's words, the way they describe themselves. Two of the variables, children and education, are compatible with the official statistics. But the others are not and can be explored only through oral history.

Finnegan (1992) argues that in oral history methodology, the researcher takes an active role by drawing sources from people's knowledge and experience. Bornet (1992) suggests that this method also involves interpersonal interaction and communication skills, which allow an understanding of social inequalities in relation to gender, class and race.

It is my hope that this oral field data will add to feminist consciousness, in exchange for the knowledge that I was able to gain from the women I interviewed, who helped me to produce this research, and that this type of research will eventually lead to a change in social relations and theoretical assumptions in the interests of women. I also hope that this book can be used to inform policy proposals, to improve women's lives and eventually lead to the promotion of women's status.

Social Differentiation among Women

The role of class and the overlap between secularity and religious adherence played a significant role in the analysis of women's employment. Within Iranian studies the phrases 'working class' and 'middle class' are widely used without adequate analysis. They are also used by my interviewees to express their social differentiation. These phrases are similar to Weberian stratification on the basis of the occupations of individuals and their families. Although I use these phrases in this book, I understand them in the context of the broad Marxian definition of class in relation to exploitation and social relations. This is because my interviewees are divided into two categories: wage-earners and non-wage-earners.

The wage-earners included twenty-seven state employees – nine nurses, five schoolteachers, four bank clerks, three secretaries, three nursery-school teachers, two university lecturers, one VDU (visual display unit) operator; and twelve employees of private enterprises – four journalists, two VDU operators, two managers/supervisors, two electronic engineers, one accountant and one secretary/administrative officer. Five nurses, one accountant and one VDU operator worked in both state and private workplaces. Among the wage-earners there were also sixteen assembly-line workers: ten in a cooking-oil factory, two in pharmaceuticals, two in a biscuit factory and two in electronics.

The twenty-five non-wage-earners included: ten petty commodity producers and traders buying cheaply from the coupon rationing system and selling expensively in the black market, either directly or by producing food and other commodities for sale; nine rural agricultural workers/carpet-weavers – unpaid family workers whose products were sold by the male members of their families; and six voluntary workers. Two of the agricultural workers/carpet-weavers moved between unpaid family work and waged employment teaching at their local schools.

Some considered themselves middle class and others working class. But in both cases they have the same relationship to the system of social production: they are dependent on selling their labour power for their livelihood. However, what distinguishes them from each other is the degree of access to material resources and the constraint imposed on them by religious ideology. These distinctions determine women's responses to employment opportunities and their mode of resistance to state ideology.

In Iran, as in other developing countries, different methods of mobilising and organising labour in production are evident; as the wage labour market developed, unwaged labour persisted. As argued by Bernstein (1994), Bernstein, Johnson and Thomas (1992) and Crow, Thorpe et al. (1988: 38–41), the transformation of developing countries from pre-capitalism to capitalism in the nineteenth and twentieth centuries took place as part of a global process and led to the establishment of forms of production based on proletarian labour (capitalist production), semi-proletarian labour (combines production using own means of production with waged labour) and petty commodity production (household labour).

Among my interviewees, some of the wage-earners are *karmand* (middle- to high-status workers) and others are *kargar* (low-status workers). Those categorised as *karmand* generally identify themselves as 'middle class' and *kargar* generally 'working class'. However, urbanisation and family status can alter the class of individuals or families. For example, two teachers in rural areas who move between waged labour (as teachers) and unwaged labour (as unpaid agricultural workers/carpet-weavers) consider themselves *kargar* and working class rather than teachers; *karmand* or middle class. All the petty commodity producers and traders in Tehran, despite their relative poverty, consider themselves middle class.

The terms *karmand* and *kargar* are local perceptions of economic status and occupational categories defined by the labour laws. Individuals and families, according to these status and categories, have different degrees of access to money, property, education, prestige. These categories also determine the *tabaghe* (social status) of an individual or a family, and become social issues affecting marriage choices, where people live, how they dress and how they furnish their homes. These local perceptions of working class and middle class are similar to the Weberian explanation of occupational categories. This view has been criticised from a Marxist point of view for being descriptive on the basis of a sociological framework of ideas about stratification and not providing a satisfactory explanation of the processes of class formation, exploitative relations of production and social relations (Callinicos 1983). The sociological approach to stratification has also been criticised from a gender and class perspective for seeing the family, rather than the individual, as the basic unit of class composition based on the occupation of the male head of household (Barrett 1988: 124–5; Acker 1973).

Marx (1956: 33) and Marxists (for example, Callinicos 1983 and Kay 1979) define class with reference to ownership and control of means of production. From this point of view, the proletariat is defined as being completely dependent on wages; and class is a social relationship through which one group exploits another within the process of production rather than a question of what their occupation is (Cohen 1978: 73–7).

The expansion of state employment and service industries in relation to manufacturing industries in the second part of this century, in both industrialised and industrialising countries, has led to debates within Marxism about the underlying relationship between capital and waged labour. For example, Offe (1985), Lukes (1984), Bauman (1982), Gorz (1982), Hobsbawm (1981) and Poulantzas (1975 and 1987) have argued that state employees and unproductive manual workers who circulate commodities and do not create surplus value are not part of the working class but of the new petty bourgeoisie.

Other writers, such as Wright (1989), Callinicos (1983), Mandel (1978: 38–46) and Braverman (1974) have argued that both productive and unproductive workers are subject to the same fundamental constraints: non-ownership of means of production; lack of direct access to the means of livelihood; insufficient money to purchase the means of livelihood without more or less continuous sale of labour power. They are also exploited in the same way: both have unpaid labour extracted from them. In the case of productive labour, unpaid labour time is appropriated directly as surplus value, whereas in the case of unproductive labour it is appropriated indirectly. Therefore all kinds of labour that contributes directly or indirectly to the process of social production is productive. The rigid application of surplus value as the criterion by which to judge labour productive or unproductive ignores the contribution of many workers to social reproduction who may not produce surplus value directly (Kay 1979: 133)

I will, therefore, argue that this second Marxian explanation can provide a more satisfactory analysis of class formation in relation to exploitation and social relations than the Weberian explanation of occupational categories. But from a gender and class perspective, Marxist analysis is also open to criticism. For example, Marx aggregates individuals into the family unit in the same way as the sociological theory of stratification (Barrett 1988: 126), as he sees the typical waged labourer as male and women and children as substitutes for the male labourer (Marx 1980: 395).

As Mies (1994: 113) argues, in the process of proletarianisation 'men are defined as wage earners and breadwinners'. Therefore a large number of women workers in developing countries are dependent on a male breadwinner; their work is not remunerated by a wage; their work is invisible in the statistics and is not protected by labour law and they cannot be easily unionised. It is important, therefore, to analyse the nature of women's relationship to the wage, domestic work and class structure (Mackintosh 1989: 163–79; Barrett 1988: 134; Gardiner 1977; Coulson, Magas and Wainwright 1975). This approach allows a historical analysis of gender relations within the context of class formation and class structure. From this perspective, self-employed workers and family workers are part of the working class; although they may not be involved in the production of surplus value directly, they are dependent upon the sale of their labour power for survival (Gardiner 1977: 157–8).

Taking these arguments into consideration, I have borrowed from Marx and Marxists the broad definition of the working class, which recognises different status such as *kargar* and *karmand*, rather than using the Weberian explanation of strata.

Karmands earn more than *kargars*. Marx recognised that some kinds of labour cost more to produce and that processes of supply and demand determine their remuneration. Hence higher-paid salary-earners could also be thought of as wage-labourers because 'the value of their labour power and their wages are determined as those of other wage earners, i.e. by the cost of production and reproduction of his specific labour power, not by the product of his labour power' (1971: 292). Therefore waged labour may have a variety of relationships to the ownership and control of capital, and state employees may not be in the same position as employees of capitalist firms.

Conclusion

These are the theoretical and practical issues raised in the production of this study. This research into women's hitherto unrecorded experiences aimed to capture the most important features of Iranian women's work and home life, which has affected, and been affected by, state ideology, economic circumstances and gender relations. The validity of the oral evidence has been checked as much as possible with the documentary evidence.

This combination of sources has enabled me to construct an accurate picture of women's employment, and to understand the social relations between the genders from the participants' point of view, and their strategies to cope with ideological constraints. Most importantly this approach has enabled me to put forward an alternative view of women and employment in Iran, and provided a framework within which to consider the academic debate on state, capital, class, patriarchy and feminism in developing countries. A critical analysis of the debates and theories and their application to the Iranian situation revealed the importance of the role of the state. As will be argued in the following chapters, the role of the state was crucial in determining the sexual division of labour and patriarchal gender relations; nevertheless, it was also dynamic and contradictory, as under economic pressure and women's resistance the state had to change its ideological position.

Notes

1. For a critical assessment of gender studies and scholarship on Iran, see De Groot 1996.
2. In feminist literature, the term 'gender' is defined to mean culturally and socially constructed categories of male and female, as opposed to 'sex', which is biologically given (Elson and Pearson 1984; Mackintosh 1984; Rubin 1975; Oakley 1972). Gender roles and gender relations are connected to the distribution of power within society (Kandiyoti 1996: 6–7). I use the terms 'feminists' and 'feminism' in their broadest sense. Feminists are activists, scholars and writers who are concerned with the oppressive, unequal man–woman relationship in the home, at work and in society and who want to change it (Paidar 1996; Mies 1986: 6–43). Feminism is used to refer to a number of schools of thought: secular feminism, Muslim feminism, socialist feminism, Marxist feminism, radical feminism.
3. This debate was pioneered by Ester Boserup's (1987) study of women in the process of economic development and is still the dominant debate. For a critical review of this debate see Pearson 1994, 1992; Kabeer 1994; Beneria and Sen 1981; Whitehead 1979; and Humphrey 1987.
4. For this discussion see Walby 1990; Mies 1986; Elson and Pearson 1984; and Mackintosh (1984).
5. For this debate see Sargent (1981), and on the specific experiences of women of the impact of capitalism and patriarchy in developing countries see Tinker 1990; Ward 1990; Agarwal 1988; Sen and Grown 1987; Beneria and Roldan 1987; Mies 1986; and Nash and Fernandez Kelly 1985.
6. For this debate see Chhachhi 1991 and Moghadam 1993b.

7. For this discussion see Kandiyoti 1991.

8. For a critical review of feminist theories in relation to women's experiences in developing countries see Goetz 1991.

9. Throughout the last three decades feminist researchers have challenged the way social sciences have analysed women's issues. The starting point is the criticism of traditional methods of analysis, which are male-biased: that is, the questions raised and the ways set up to answer those questions are not derived from the perspective of female experiences. Stanley 1990 and Harding 1987.

10. Squires (1989), Graham (1983), Morgan (1981), Oakley (1981) and Stacey (1981) have argued that qualitative method is more appropriate for counting women's contribution and analysing the social relationships between women and men in the home and at work. Furthermore, the use of qualitative research has the advantage of reflecting women's experiences as a whole, including their paid and unpaid work in and for the family.

11. Harding (1987) and Jayaratne (1983) have argued that the appropriate use of both quantitative and qualitative methods have also been considered satisfactory to promote feminist theory and goals.

Chapter 2

Continuity and Change: A Historical Approach

The experience of the 1979 revolution and the process of Islamisation of the state and society resulted from the socio-economic and socio-political development of Iran in this century. The economic and political structures developed during the Pahlavi period entailed an interrelationship and interdependency between economic development and religious ideology. Industrialisation created new social classes and accelerated the process of proletarianisation. Female paid employment became crucial for the families, especially in the 1960s and 1970s. But cultural values based on Shii Islam ideology persisted, creating conflict and obstacles on the path of women's participation in the public sphere, particularly paid employment.

In this chapter I want to assess the way in which gender is historically implicated in the political economy of Iran. The early stage of capitalist development, changing class structure, social and political reforms, and how women related to these changes in the pre-Pahlavi period are important factors, as they laid the foundation of continuity and change in the pre- and post-Pahlavi era. But I will concentrate on the Pahlavi period, and analyse how men and women have been incorporated differently into economic, political and social processes. The pre-1979 period has been divided, therefore, into two periods of socio-economic and socio-political development (1925–60 and 1960–79). The focus is on two different aspects of these periods (gender and the economic processes and gender and politics). During the period 1925–60 Iran rapidly integrated into the world economy under Reza Shah and the British and later American domination; while 1960–79 saw the oil boom economy under Mohammad Reza Pahlavi and American domination, ending with the 1979 revolution and the establishment of the Islamic state. I shall analyse the role of the state and its social and political institutions in determining gender relations within the Iranian economy and society by looking into the processes of continuity as well as change. At different points in the modern history of Iran, the interaction between the state, Shii Islam, capitalism and imperialism affected gender relations. Women of different classes and with different levels of religious commitment participated in economic and political activities, and at different levels struggled against the patriarchal state and its institutions. They achieved some change. However, as a result of the interdependency and interrelationship between economic development and religious ideology, and despite economic and political change, the state perpetuated female subordination.

Early Capitalist Development, Class Structure and Women's Responses

Capitalist development in Iran was the result of the need of the European capitalist market to import Iranian goods, and to export European manufactured goods into Iran, in the nineteenth century. Iran was never colonised or formally ruled by a foreign power. The rivalry between the Russian and British empires allowed Iran to maintain its independence (Tabari 1983: 53). Nevertheless, Iran's integration into the world system, although it had its own characteristics, shared those features of uneven economic development experienced by countries colonised by foreign powers.

For example, in this period, the population of Iran was classified into four social groups: the landed aristocracy, the propertied middle class, urban wage-earners and (the vast majority) the rural population (Abrahamian 1982: 33–4). However, British and Russian trading activities in Iran led to the decline of landed proprietors, as they gradually became large-scale profiteers, disposing of cash crops such as cotton, opium, silk, dried fruits and nuts in foreign markets. As a result the economy was transformed from being based largely on transactions in kind into a monetised economy. The influence of western capitalism meant that industries were destroyed through trade and the import of foreign goods; on the other hand, this influence accelerated the growth of the urban population, of non-agricultural activities and of commercial agriculture. The influence of the global market changed pre-existing patterns of economic and social life through the reorganisation of labour into proletarians, semi-proletarians and petty commodity producers. These persist today, characterising uneven development in the context of global capitalism.

> If we view the global history of capitalism, we see that it has absorbed, created and combined many diverse social forms in the course of its uneven and contradictory development. For example, capitalism is usually characterized by the employment of wage labour (or full proletarian-isation) but other labour regimes can and do co-exist under capitalism. (Bernstein, Johnson and Thomas 1992: 193–4)

Women played an important economic role in this period. Before the discovery of oil in 1914, the main exports were agricultural products and handicrafts. In rural areas, rice, butter, dried fruits, and tea were produced exclusively by women, and women had an important role in the production of wheat, barley, tobacco, cotton, hides, skins, raw silk, drugs, dyes and manufactured silk, wool and cotton (Issawi 1971: 132–4). In urban areas, capitalist relations emerged between the weaver and those who ran and controlled carpet-making. The mass of the workers, mainly women and children, were paid a wage below subsistence and controlled neither the raw material nor the finished product (Seyf 1994/95: 190–201). Thus women were among the early proletarians, semi-proletarians and petty commodity producers.

Towards the end of the nineteenth century, carpet-weaving became an important manufacturing industry, employing a large urban workforce. But the most common form of organisation remained small-scale domestic production, where women were the main labour force. Women also remained solely responsible for the repro-duction of the family and the household despite demand for their labour, which brought cash for their families, created profits for the foreign and indigenous owners and revenue for the country (Seyf 1994/95: 143–56; Issawi 1971: 304–5).

In 1914 the economic organisation of Iran began to change. With the discovery of large quantities of oil, Britain began to exploit it through the Anglo-Persian Oil Company (Issawi 1971: 316–22). Although Iran gradually benefited from a share of its oil production, a significant contribution to Iran's economy still came from agriculture and handicrafts, produced largely by women (Kazemi 1980: 32–3). In this period, Clara Rice, a member of a Christian mission who travelled widely in Iran, recorded the importance of women's unpaid work in rural areas as agriculturalists, pastoralists and carpet-weavers, as well as producing food and clothes for their families (Azad 1987/88: 46–9, 63, 171–81).

Social and Political Reforms and Women's Responses

Economic development in Iran led to social and political changes. A number of students, government officials and merchants associated with the landed aristocracy and the propertied middle class travelled to Europe and were impressed by the achievements of Europe's industrial revolutions. This instigated social and political change, as these middle classes pressurised the Qajar Shahs to centralise and strengthen the state, creating a new army, secular courts and schools on the European model (Bakhash 1978: 1–3). However, the *olama*, who were part of the landed aristocracy or the propertied middle class, opposed the modernisation of education and the courts as these changes would have undermined their traditional role, including collecting religious taxes, and their positions as judges, educators and guild leaders. Hence a conflict of class interest was created within this group: some were in favour of social and economic modernisation; others were against, favouring a return to religion and the *Sharia*.

During the second half of the nineteenth century Britain and Russia imposed their banks upon Iran and began indirect exploitation by acquiring 'concessions' to collect taxes and to extract and market raw materials and agricultural products, in exchange for an often paltry sum paid to the Qajar Shahs. In 1890 a British company obtained the monopoly over the production, sale and export of tobacco from Iran, and this concession produced a massive wave of popular discontent. Two opposing forces with different objectives

united against foreign domination: the producers of tobacco and
the merchants who exported it were in favour of Iran's integration
into the world market, but without foreign domination, while the
olama objected to foreign domination because their economic, political and social power were declining as a result of that integration
(Algar 1969; Keddie 1966).

This alliance called for a boycott of tobacco. Strikes and street
demonstrations made the anti-concession campaign highly successful. Women participated in street demonstrations for the first time.
Even the wives of the Shah and the women in the harems were
influential in this mass anti-imperialist movement. They boycotted
smoking and broke their pipes. The Shah was forced to cancel the
concession (Hendessi 1990: 5; Bahar 1983: 172; Bayat-Philipp 1978:
297).

The experience of the anti-tobacco uprising led to the Constitutional Revolution of 1906–11, which had an important influence on
the development of women's political participation. The Constitutional Revolution was also won out of the alliance of the two opposing forces: secularist merchants who were involved in trade,
money-lending and the establishment of industries, supported by
liberal intellectuals, demanded a fair chance against foreign capital,
and fundamental economic, political and ideological change; and
the olama demanded an end to foreign domination and the return of
religious power and tradition (Keddie 1966; Browne 1910). In the
literature, the former is referred to as the modern middle class and
the latter as the traditional middle class (Najmabadi 1991: 49–66;
Abrahamian 1982: 58–69). Each of them sought the support of
women across the society.

> Women were considered as significant to the nation because of their
> role as biological reproducers of the nation, educators of children, trans-
> mitters of culture and participants in national life. Their position in any
> society, it followed, was central to the definition of that society. A social
> and political redefinition of Iranian society, therefore, had to entail a
> reorganisation of women's position. (Paidar 1997: 73)

This gave rise to a diverse women's movement in Iran, as some
women supported the modernists and others the olama. But their
collective political actions created space and opportunity for women

to organise themselves and participate in political movements (Paidar 1997: 74).

The Shah's reaction to the constitutional struggle was to disrupt this alliance by constructing one of his own with the *olama*, offering the closure of the western-style schools that educated girls (Sanasarian 1982: 18–24; Nashat 1983: 22–4). These schools became centres for raising women's consciousness in Iran. Through these schools a small number of young women from the upper and middle classes learned about French women's involvement in the Paris Commune, British women's fight for the vote and Russian women's struggle against the Tsar. These stories had great importance for women in Iran during this period and were repeated from woman to woman, in family circles, in mosques and even in public baths (Nahid 1981: 16).

During the constitutional movement, women graduates of these schools established girls' schools themselves. Although they were opposed by the Islamic clergy, they continued and greatly developed women's consciousness in Iran (Sanasarian 1982: 39; Nahid 1981: 19). Women wearing the *chador* participated in sit-ins and demonstrations and fought for women's rights (Bahar 1983: 174, 188; Abrahamian 1982: 109). Women's organisations and newspapers also played an important role in establishing constitutional government and ending foreign intervention and domination (Paidar 1997: 66, 92; Hendessi 1990: 6; Jayawardena 1986: 64–5; Sanasarian 1982: 21; Bayat-Philipp 1978: 298, 307).

For many women the constitutional movement was to bring about their emancipation through economic development and progress associated with western democracy. Their demands were education for women, and the abolition of seclusion and early marriage. This early women's movement was secular, viewing Islam as traditionalist and backward; it glorified pre-Islamic Iran and Babism, a reformist movement (1820–50) which had challenged Shii Islam (Paidar 1996: 52).

Although the majority of these early feminists took sides with their men and avoided direct confrontation with Islam, they blamed men within the family and society for women's subordination Adamiyat and Nategh 1978: 20–27). They demanded greater social justice, freedom of trade and rights of personal property, the reduction of unjust taxes, a higher status for women, limits on polygamy, a prohibition on violence against women and measures for their education (Jayawardena 1986: 61; Bahar 1983: 171; Keddie 1981: 50; Bayat-Philipp 1978: 296).

The constitution was won and the Qajar dynasty was defeated. But, as a result of the persistence of the power of Islamic ideology and the secularists' concessions to the Islamists, women's rights were sacrificed. Alongside criminals and the insane, the female population of Iran was denied the right to vote. But women's struggle continued through the establishment of girls' schools, women's newspapers and societies (Nashat 1983: 23–4; Sanasarian 1982: 42–3).

With the outbreak of the First World War, British and Russian troops occupied almost all of Iran, creating widespread popular opposition to the occupying powers. During this period, political organisations, women's groups, trade unions and radical newspapers appeared throughout the country. In the north of Iran, popular support for nationalist and communist movements expanded rapidly. After the Russian Revolution, the Bolsheviks quickly abandoned Tsarist privileges in Iran. This concentrated popular anger against the British, who retained control in oil-rich southern Iran (Zabih 1966: 1–35; Degras 1950: 28–9). Women supporters and activists in the nationalist *jangali* (forest people) and communist movements organised women's groups and produced several women's publications and newspapers during this period of anti-imperialist agitation (Abrahamian 1982: 128; Sanasarian 1982; Nahid 1981: 111–13).

The women's movement of the 1920s was different from the constitutional women's movement. During the constitutional period the women's movement was part of the nationalist movement. In the 1920s the women's movement in Iran achieved a degree of independence from political parties (Paidar 1997: 91). It was a small, secularist movement pioneered by modern middle-class women in association with the nationalists and communists. This movement was diverse in its ideological struggle, but through its political activities it demanded equal opportunities in education and political rights for women, was against child marriage and polygamy, against the *Chador* and Islamic laws, and participated in the fight against imperialist domination. Although those in the movement were a minority, they achieved a degree of reform – especially in the area of education – which was beneficial to the majority of women. But an unholy alliance between the clergy and secularists made it impossible for them to develop fully and achieve more.

To conclude, the process of economic development and class formation was part of a global process which took place under foreign intervention, imperialist domination and the influence of the Shii clergy. This created uneven socio-economic development. The new social classes remained differentiated in the degree of economic integration and level of religious influence. All these factors affected gender issues. Women played an important role in the economy, but in rural areas they remained predominantly unpaid workers, while in urban industrial centres they constituted the low-paid, even though their products were sold in national and international markets and the state and the family benefited from their economic participation. A small but significant number of women actively participated in nationalist and communist movements. They raised feminist issues in relation to the family, education and veiling. Their activities laid the foundation for future struggle for women's emancipation.

Gender and Economic Processes under the Pahlavi, 1925–60

In December 1925, the Qajar King was deposed and Reza Pahlavi declared himself the Shah of the Pahlavi dynasty. Under the influence of the British he was committed to building a modern state and economy. Iranian economic development in this period largely centred on the development of infrastructure. These developments were linked to the Shah's desire effectively to control the country through the army and to the desire of British capital to exploit the oil resources with greater ease, but they also laid the foundation for industrial development in this period. Industrial development under Reza Shah began during the global depression of the 1930s, when the terms of trade were in Iran's favour, as oil was exported in return for imported capital goods. The industrialisation drive increased government revenue through taxation and the growth of oil income. The government introduced high tariffs and income tax and imposed state monopolies in some consumer goods, to increase state revenue (Abrahamian 1982: 135–65).

Rapid integration into the world economy created new social classes. The landed aristocracy and the propertied middle class declined in economic, social and political power. The modern middle class, who were in favour of secular changes, were attracted to Reza Shah's modernisation of the economy and society and became the new bourgeoisie and the professional salary-earners. They were encouraged by Reza Shah to participate actively in the growing state bureaucracy. The traditional middle class, who were opposed to modernisation, lost much of their economic and political power and this created intense hatred for Reza Shah.

In this period women were encouraged to go to universities, become teachers and work for the growing state sector. The state bureaucracy grew fast and absorbed a small number of modern middle-class women (Najmabadi 1991: 54). However, the process of industrialisation and the development of a market economy, which might have required female labour-force participation, was limited. In the 1920s and 1930s, 79 per cent of the population still lived in rural areas (Bharier 1977: 335). Agriculture and household-centred industries remained important economically, and women's unpaid work in agriculture and pastoral nomadic activities continued (Halliday: 1979: 14).

When the economic depression reached Iran, low wages, long working hours and bad labour conditions caused widespread industrial discontent. Reza Shah's state increasingly faced gender, class and ethnic opposition. In 1941, Britain and Russia invaded Iran, fearing Reza Shah's pro-German attitude. The occupying powers forced the Shah to leave the country and to abdicate in favour of his son Mohammad Reza.

Industrialisation and economic development, especially in the 1940s and 1950s, which involved the provision of better healthcare and education, led to a decrease in the mortality rate, while the birth rate remained high. Iran's population increased from 9,860,000 in 1900 to 19,880,000 in 1955, and the urban population increased from 21 per cent to 30 per cent, as a result of migration from rural areas to industrialising cities (Bharier 1977: 335).

Sectoral statistical data exist only from 1956 onwards. Very little detailed information about women's economic participation is available, but there is a general consensus that in the 1940s–1950s, 90 per cent of the population were either nomadic pastoralists or engaged in agricultural work (Halliday 1979: 14). Only 200,000 people worked in industry, of whom 120,000 were working with modern technology (Razaghi 1988/9: 24). In this period, 40 per cent of revenue came from the agricultural sector, 10 per cent from the oil industry, 20 per cent from other industries and the rest from unspecified sources (Behnam 1977: 47–8). Therefore, until the 1950s, the significant contribution to Iran's economy came from agriculture, where women played an important role in the production of food and labour-intensive goods in household-centred industries. According to the statistics, in 1956–57 over 50 per cent of the population lived in rural areas. As a result of the high birth rate, lack of sanitation and malnutrition, the female mortality rate was higher than the male. As in most developing countries, the female population was 2 per cent smaller than the male population (Iran Statistical Yearbook 1996: 35).

In 1941, within the paid labour market 13,000 women workers were counted. This figure increased to 573,000 in 1956. Although child labour was prohibited, many children, the majority of them girls, worked in factories. Child labour in 1956 did not differ much from the 1930s. Women were mostly employed in carpet-weaving, textile and spinning factories; in factories making matches, glass and cardboard boxes; in tea factories, cotton cleaning and gunny sack factories; and in the embroidery industries. In the service sector they remained in the lowest grades of cleaning, catering, education and health. These women were categorised as unskilled labourers and therefore received a much lower wage than men (Afshar 1989: 43–44; Sanasarian 1982: 97).

To summarise briefly, under Reza Pahlavi development took place through state-building and the modernisation of the economy and society. Development indicators such as provision of health, education and employment reflected a change in the social and economic make-up of Iranian society. Women were encouraged to participate in paid work, especially in the state sector. Nevertheless in the 1940s and 1950s Iran's economy was still based on agriculture; women constituted the majority of the unpaid workforce in rural areas and in urban areas they remained poorly paid.

Gender and politics

Under the early years of Reza Shah's rule, some women's organisations and publications continued their activities. Afaghe Parsa, a
member of Anjomane Nesvane Vatankhah (Patriotic Women's League),
represented Iranian women at the International Congress of Women
in Paris in 1926. *Alame Nesvan* (Women's Universe) magazine was
published in 1930 and encouraged Iranian women's participation
and representation at the Asian women's conference to be held in
India in 1931. In 1927, in Rasht in the north of Iran, four women,
among them Roshanak Noodoost, set up Anjoman Payke Saadat (the
Messenger of Prosperity Organisation), published a magazine and
established a girls' school, both called *Payke Saadat*, and declared 8
March as Women's Day in Iran. In the same year Zandokhte Shirazi,
a poet and writer, founded the Majmae Enghelabe Zanan (Revolutionary Women's League) in Shiraz, in the south of Iran, and in
1931–32 published *Dokhtarane Iran* (Iranian Women) newspaper (Sanasarian 1982: 54; Nahid 1981: 111–13)

The founders of these organisations and publications were middle-
class women, but they were conscious of, and sought to improve,
the degrading conditions of working-class women. Under the
dictatorial regime of Reza Shah the power of the Islamic clergy
declined. However, the power of Islamic ideology on issues relating
to women and the family remained strong (Paidar 1997: 120–23).
Most feminists in this period, therefore, concentrated on female
education, health, and unequal marriage and divorce laws. They only
indirectly argued about the question of the veil and women's right
to vote. Some leading members in this period were from Muslim
families and considered the teaching of Islam necessary. But they
were critical of the way women were treated. They argued that child
marriage and not allowing women to be educated and to participate
in public life was unIslamic. Other leaders and organisations such
as Nesvane Vatankhah, under the leadership of Mohtaram Iskandari,
a socialist, mobilised rallies and demonstrations against the clergy
and Islamic law (Sanasarian 1982: 46–7, 54; Abrahamian 1982: 128).

Soon Reza Shah's power was consolidated and all independent
organisations, including women's organisations, were suppressed.
In 1935 he ordered the establishment of the Kanoone Banovan
(Ladies' Centre). The aim was not to promote equal rights but to

create one women's organisation under the control of the state. He allowed only charity work, sports clubs and adult literacy for women. During 1935–36, as part of his modernisation of society, he campaigned to force women to abandon the veil in all public places. In 1937, the celebration of 8 March was prohibited, and 7 January was declared Women's Day, the first official day of the public unveiling campaign. Women's responses varied; many considered this to be a case not of women's emancipation but of police repression. But many celebrated the occasion. Parvin Etesami (1907–1941), for example, a well-known woman poet who longed to see this happening, celebrated the occasion with a famous poem (Jayawardena 1986: 69; Bayat-Philipp 1978: 306).

There was very little resistance to Reza Shah's autocratic state, partly because individuals feared for their lives and organisations feared repression, but also because many feminist leaders of the previous period were disappointed with the secular constitutionalists who made concessions to the *olama* and, as a result, sacrificed female suffrage and reform of women's education and employment. Many welcomed Reza Shah's limited reforms of education, modernisation of the economy, and political and social changes generally. Seddighe Doulatabadi, the founder of Sazeman Sherkate Khavatin, became the president of the Kanoone Banovan in 1937, and Fakhrozma Argum, a member of Nesvane Vatankhah, also joined the centre and edited two periodicals – *Banovan* (Ladies) and *Ayandeh Iran* (Iran's Future). For these women, who had long struggled for education and employment, on their own and without the support of their male counterparts, Reza Shah's limited reforms were a blessing (Najmabadi 1991: 57–8). For example, the number of girls' schools had increased from 41 in 1910 to 870 in 1933, and the enrolment of girls from 2,167 in 1910 to about 50,000 in 1933 (Sanasarian 1982: 62).

Reza Shah's reforms were based on massive repression of all political groups, from communists to liberals, of protesting clergy, trade unions, women's organisations and minority nationalities (Najmabadi 1991: 52; Abrahamian 1982: 135–65). Iran's population has always been only two-thirds Persian and Farsi-speaking (the official language); the remaining third comprises other nationalities and ethnic groups (Abrahamian 1982: 12). Under Reza Shah's state these minorities were denied linguistic, cultural and national rights, in addition to the denial of civil rights to everybody. As a result a long tradition has existed of fighting the central state authority.

The aim of Reza Shah's reform was to centralise state power, which meant keeping the clergy and religious institutions under strict control. Despite this, the reforms in relation to women and the family remained ambiguous and not necessarily in contradiction with basic *Sharia* law. For example, the age of marriage was left to depend upon local interpretation of the age of puberty; a wife had the right to object to her husband marrying another woman, and the man had to inform his wife if he intended to do so. But in many parts of the country civil courts did not exist and the local clergy dealt with marriage and divorce issues according to their own interpretation of the law. The law continued to regard men as superior, and they retained their Muslim privileges of having up to four wives at a time and divorcing at will. A man was still recognised as the legal head of the family and enjoyed more favourable inheritance rights. Women remained deprived of the right to vote and could not stand for election. Nevertheless, these limited reforms led to a long-lasting political conflict between Shii leaders and the Pahlavi regime. At the heart of this conflict was the issue of women's unveiling and their participation in public life (Sanasarian 1982: 60–61; Yeganeh 1982: 32)

After Reza Shah's abdication in 1941, the power of the state declined. Women's publications and organisations began to flourish and women's role in social and political activities expanded: *Zanane Pishraw* (Progressive Women) was published by Sedigheh Ganjeh; *Ghiayme Zanan* (Women's Revolt) by Soghra Aliabadi; *Hoghughe Zanan* (Women's Rights) by Ebtehaj Mostahag; *Azadi Zanan* (The Emancipation of Women) by Zafardokht Ardalan; *Zane Mobarez* (Militant Women) by Kobra Saremi; *Banu* (The Lady) by Nayereh Saidi; *Banuye Iran* (Iran's Lady) by Malekeh Etezadi (Paidar 1997: 125–8).

Badrulmoluk Bamdad founded Jamiyate Zanane Iran (the Iranian Women's League) and published *Zane Emruz* (Today's Woman); Safiyeh Firuz founded Hezbe Zanane Iran (the Iranian Women's Party) and Published *Zanane Iran* (Iran's Women). Fatimah Sayyah, the first woman professor at Tehran University, worked as a writer and a journalist and represented Iran at the United Nations. She edited *Zanane Iran* and raised issues of women's suffrage and their right to education and employment (Bahar 1983: 180). In 1945 the Iranian Women's Party became the National Council of Women. These organisations and publications campaigned for women's education, legal rights, equality of rights in marriage and divorce and women's suffrage. Representatives of these organisations attended international conferences in Paris (1946), New York (1946), Delhi (1947), Beirut (1949) and Geneva (1953). A number of professional, religious and charity organisations were also established to promote women's health and education (Paidar 1997: 128).

Tashkilateh Zanane Iran (the Organisation of Iranian Women) was the biggest women's organisation;[1] it later became known as Jame-heye Demokratike Zanan (the Society of Democratic Women). Its leading members were Zahra and Taj Iskandari, Maryam Firouz, Khadijeh Keshawarz, Akhtar Kambakhsh and Badrimonir Alavi, associated with the secular women's movement of the previous period. It published the monthly magazine *Bidarie Ma* (Our Awakening). It had branches in major cities and their active members travelled to rural areas. They organised public meetings and, through consciousness-raising activities, raised issues in relation to prostitution, unpaid women's work and child labour; and demanded women's rights to social and political participation, education, health, employment, child-care facilities and equal pay (Bahar 1983: 180; Yeganeh 1982: 33).

During 1951–53 women supporters of the nationalist movement and activists within Jebhe Melli (The National Front) played an important role in support of the nationalist government of Mossadegh by selling national government bonds to raise funds. Jebhe Melli's members and supporters consisted of both the modern and the traditional middle classes. These women's organisations were independent of the state, but closely related to different political parties; therefore their activities ranged from campaigning and raising issues in relation to Iran's independence from foreign domination to socialism and to promoting specific feminist issues.

Despite their diversity, their collective activities influenced the reform of the labour law, which, had it been implemented, could have been beneficial to the women who constituted a large number of agricultural and handicraft workers. For example, in 1946 factory work was limited to forty-eight hours a week. Overtime was made voluntary. Children could work no more than six hours a day, and no children less than ten years old were allowed to work in factories. Women were to have twelve weeks' paid maternity leave. A minimum wage was established based on subsistence costs for a family of four (Keddie 1981: 121).

In 1952 the National Council of Women, which was a confederation of various women's groups, wrote a petition demanding political and economic rights for women, especially the right to vote. They collected 100,000 signatures and sent them to Prime Minister Mossadegh, the Majles and the United Nations. But pressure from the religious wing of the Jebhe Melli and the clergy ensured that women were not granted the right to vote under Mossadegh's premiership (Sanasarian 1982: 75; Abrahamian 1982: 336).

Nevertheless, during the CIA coup d'état of 1953, which overthrew Mossadegh, many women, under the leadership of different women's organisations, fought side by side with men against the victorious forces, and some were killed. After the defeat of the nationalist and communist movements, Mohammad Reza Shah crushed all opposition, including women's organisations and publications. In 1958, Shoraye Aliye Jamiate Zanan (the High Council of Women's Organisation) was formed under the presidency of Ashraf Pahlavi, Mohammad Reza Shah's twin sister. Some feminist activists of the previous period joined this organisation in order to be able to carry on the pressure for reforms on women's issues. For example, Nurol Hoda Manganeh, a member of the old Nesvane Vatankhah, joined this organisation, edited Bibi magazine in 1955, and wrote for various periodicals and journals on women's issues (Sanasarian 1982: 83–5; Yeganeh 1982: 32).

A number of women's publications continued to be produced under the supervision of the state: Ettellaat Banovan (Women's Information), Nedaye Zanan (Women's Call), Banuye Iran (Iran's Lady) and Zanane Iran (Women of Iran). A number of women's organisations also continued their activities with the general consent of the government: Jamiyat Rah Now (the New Path League), the League of Women Supporters of the Declaration of Human Rights, the Association of Women Lawyers and Federation of Women's Organisations. These organisations, despite political repression, campaigned for women's rights, especially the right to vote (Paidar 1997: 134–7).

In general, therefore, during the period 1925–60 the authoritarian Pahlavi state did not allow women's independent organisations and actions. However, in response to any weakening of the state women took the opportunity to organise and struggle for reforms. Despite a drive to secularise the state, *Sharia* remained untouched in laws concerning women, especially in the area of morality, marriage, divorce and family relationships.

Gender and Economic Processes, 1960–79

The 1960s and 1970s saw Iran's economy and society transformed on a much greater scale than in previous periods. Nevertheless women were incorporated into the economic processes differently from men.

In June 1963, after months of mass strikes, demonstrations and university occupations, where thousands were injured and some killed, Mohammad Reza Shah (the Shah) launched a programme of reform known as the White Revolution of the Shah and the People. The White Revolution further transformed the Iranian economy and society. Its programme (land reform, industrialisation, nationalisation of natural resources, female suffrage, and the formation of a literacy and health corps) was to provide a stable social, economic and political system. Two important social groups – medium-sized capitalist farmers and entrepreneurs – emerged who had an interest in maintaining the regime. The vastly expanded numbers of state employees, mainly in the cities, also benefited from the reforms.

Land reform did not redistribute land on a massive scale, but it established capitalist relations of production in agriculture. About 9,500 large landowners, with more than 100 hectares each, owned over 3.5 million hectares of land; tens of thousands of medium landowners, with 50–100 hectares each, and small landowners, with 30–50 hectares each, together owned close to 3 million hectares. This was done by the introduction of money through rents and loans. The landowners were provided with capital in order to employ labourers to produce for the national market (Moaddel 1991: 318).

Land reform limited the economic power of the clergy, who for centuries had relied on donations from large landowners as well as from the *bazaar* (market place). Land reform stopped a main source of their revenue, leaving them dependent on the *bazaar*, which was itself being undermined by the industrialisation of the economy. The establishment of a literacy corps, under which young men were conscripted into the army and sent as teachers into the rural areas, expanded secular education and totally undermined the role of the clergy in education.

In 1960, when the Organisation of Petroleum Exporting Countries (OPEC) was formed, Iran was the smallest producer and exporter, but by 1970 it had become the second largest in the world. Iran's share of ownership of its oil increased to 96 per cent. Iran gained ownership and control over the price and the level of its production; the oil previously owned and controlled by the oil majors. As a result oil revenue increased to US$22 billion (Halliday, 1979: 143).

The oil money was the instigator of economic development. As the recipient of oil revenues, the state became the main force for industrial growth. The Gross Domestic Product (GDP) of Iran increased tenfold between 1962 and 1974. Industrial production accounted for 15 per cent of GDP and employed around 20 per cent of the economically active population. By 1975, 60 per cent of all industrial investment was directed by the state. The state also undertook the building of infrastructure. The private sector, subsidised by the state, concentrated on light industries while foreign capital invested in areas of technology and management in both heavy and light industries. Official policy on foreign investment under the Shah's regime favoured joint ventures.

In this period, Iran's economic development was compared to that of Mexico; the country was seen as potentially a major industrial power by the end of the century (Halliday 1979: 167–8). The state, as the recipient of the oil income and the main agent of economic development, was closely linked to the western powers, especially the USA, which had both economic and political interests in Iran and throughout the region. The bourgeoisie, consisting of one thousand families, controlled key sectors of the economy and had close ties with international capital and with the Pahlavi family. They owned 85 per cent of the major private firms involved in agribusiness, banking, manufacturing, foreign trade, insurance and urban construction, and occupied positions such as senior civil servants and high-ranking military officers (Moaddel 1991: 317). Industrialisation entailed a relative decline in the role of the *bazaar*. But still a large number of merchants were engaged in the *bazaar* as wholesale traders and retailers, and controlled one-third of imports and two-thirds of retail trade (Moaddel 1991: 318). The commercialisation of agriculture and the growth of manufacturing industry speeded up the process of proletarianisation, but semi-proletarianisation and petty commodity production persisted.

Economic growth led to improvement in material welfare, especially in health, education, provision of new types of consumer goods, and the strength of the labour force (Abrahamian 1982: 426–35; Halliday, 1979: 138–73). But economic development was uneven; modern technology did not reach most industries. In textile industries, where women constituted the majority of the workforce, production remained labour-intensive and productivity remained low (Bartsch: 1977: 323–4). The process of proletarianisation intensified, but discriminated against women, who constituted a greater share of semi-skilled, unskilled and unpaid family workers. Improvement in health led to lower mortality rates. Despite better education and family planning, the population growth rate remained as high as 2.7 per cent. Despite industrialisation and urbanisation, there was widespread malnutrition, low life expectancy and high infant mortality. Half of the population lived in rural areas and females continued to number 2 per cent fewer than males (Iran Statistical Yearbook 1996: 35).

Land reform and the introduction of wage labour had little effect on the role of women as unpaid agricultural producers and carpet-weavers. In some ways women's position deteriorated. The small plots of land distributed to poor peasants were not enough for their survival; they were neither able to benefit from rent nor in a position to obtain loans, or, if they did, to pay back their debt. This led to male migration to the cities, leaving land and production to women. As is shown in Table 2.1, in the majority of cases a woman followed her husband and family or migrated in order to marry a husband chosen for her.

The family remained interconnected with the labour market, and

Table 2.1   Comparison of female and male reasons for migration in rural and urban areas, 1972

| | Urban areas | | Rural areas | |
	Male	Female	Male	Female
Looking for work	165,000	13,000	4,000	<1,000
Better work	620,000	2,000	71,000	<1,000
Job transfer	177,000	9,000	17,000	1,000
Education	24,000	3,000	1,000	0
Marriage	3,000	275,000	1,000	48,000
With family	921,000	1,506,000	104,000	133,000
Other	112,000	23,000	40,000	2,000
Total	2,022,000	1,831,000	238,000	184,000

Source: Extracted from Iran Statistical Yearbook 1977: 39.

women's choice and power of decision making were not equal to men's. Women were much more restricted than men in their job opportunities. Their triple role as mothers, wives and workers affected their chances in the labour market. The mechanisation of agriculture did not affect women's work – mainly weeding, picking, planting and harvesting – and often increased their hours, where better ploughed and irrigated land extended their responsibilities (Tabari 1982: 7).

Table 2.2 shows that despite improvement in female literacy rate, the gap between men and women was still high. Therefore males benefited from education opportunities more than females, which could explain why women were concentrated in low-paid jobs. Thus, the state and its institutions – the family, the education system and the labour market – pervade gender division and the process of perpetuation of women's subordination.

In some areas, life for women was different. Among the nomadic pastoralists, women's work remained an important part of the household economy and survival: milking, milk processing (yogurt, butter, cheese and oil), preparation of animal derivatives (skin, hair and wool), care of animals, light firewood collection, bringing of water,

Table 2.2 Comparison of female and male literacy rates in urban and rural areas, 1966–77 (per cent)

	1966/7			1976/7		
	Total	Female	Male	Total	Female	Male
Urban areas	50.4	38.3	61.4	65.4	55.6	74.4
Rural areas	15.1	4.3	25.4	30.5	17.3	43.6
All areas	29.4	17.9	40.1	47.5	35.5	58.9

Source: Calculated from Iran Statistical Yearbook 1992: 113.

gathering wild plants, baking bread, cooking and child care, weaving, spinning and dyeing the yarn. Women prepared the goods to be taken to towns by men for trade, but they did not receive any payment for their work (Beck 1978: 358–60).

In the 1970s, 13 per cent of all women over the age of twelve (1.4 million) were in paid employment. A total of 70 per cent of all cloth weaving and 72 per cent of carpet-weaving was in the rural sector (Halliday 1979: 191–3). Some 90 per cent of this workforce was female and 40 per cent of them were under the age of fifteen. They were either unpaid family workers or received very low wages; they worked in appalling conditions and were at the mercy of the middlemen who employed them (Tabari 1982: 7). In 1970, in Yazd textile mills, women were paid 90 rials (75 pence) per day, which was below subsistence level (Fischer 1978: 192–3).

Table 2.2 shows that the literacy rate amongst women was higher in urban areas than in rural areas. In urban areas the growth of industries, services and the state bureaucracy provided better employment opportunities for women. In 1974/5 the state ministries (the majority of them in urban areas) employed 297,863 workers, of which 29 per cent were female; in 1972/3 industries employing more than ten workers (the majority of them private enterprises in urban areas) employed 249,649 workers, of whom 8 per cent were women, while the small private enterprises (urban and rural) employed 6,922,000 people, of whom 9 per cent were women, the majority of them being unpaid family workers in rural households (Iran Statistical Yearbook 1977/8: 66, 386, 50).

In urban employment 200,000 were in a professional category, working in the state and service sector as doctors, engineers, architects, pharmacists, university professors and judges. Some women became parliamentary deputies, senators, ministers and ambassadors. In other occupations the proportion of women was 45 per cent in teaching, 44 per cent in clerical and administrative positions, 11 per cent in medical and paramedical positions (Najmabadi 1991: 61; Halliday 1979: 191–3).

Rapid and uneven industrial development in this period affected only a very small sector within the economy, creating regional, class and gender differentiations. In 1978, the GNP per capita was higher than US$2,000. However, 87 per cent of Iran's villages had no school, only 1 per cent had a medical facility of any sort, 40–50 per cent of the budget went on military spending and prices had risen steeply. The investment programme required a high level of imports. By 1978, non-oil exports covered only 3.1 per cent of imports, making the country's growth dependent mainly on oil exports. Imports consisted mainly of capital goods, semi-manufactured goods, food, arms, and consumption goods to satisfy the growing demand of the newly rich middle class (Abrahamian 1982: 426–35; Halliday 1979: 173).

This pattern resulted in middle-class prosperity, concentrated in a large state bureaucracy and in a service sector enjoying salary increases of over 30 per cent per year, while a lower-income group remained squeezed by high inflation, on average 15 per cent per annum between 1974 and 1978. Under these circumstances, for the majority of the population, the state was an institution which served the interests of foreign powers and the dominant classes.

By the end of 1975 the fall in oil demand, coupled with the high rate of domestic and international inflation, led to cash-flow problems. To carry out and finance its industrialisation plans, Iran had to borrow massively from the international banks. Iran then was seen as a country unable to feed large parts of its population, in massive debt to the international banks and with falling oil revenue. The ruling class embarked on an orgy of corruption and speculation, spending and making quick profits and salting away their money in foreign banks (Abrahamian 1982: 426–35; Halliday 1979: 173).

Property speculation, corruption and the hoarding of commodities led to an inflation rate of nearly 40 per cent. Rent consumed an average of one-quarter of earnings, cheap food vanished from the market, industrial production began to fall back, and official figures estimated an unemployment rate of 15 per cent, with no benefits. During this time Iran became the largest arms importer in the world. The number of American military advisers reached 24,000 and was expected to grow to about 60,000. Sazemaneh Ettellaat Va Amniat Keshvar (SAVAK, the secret police) expanded and employed over 5,300 full-time agents and a large but unknown number of part-time informers. In 1973 Tehran became the headquarters of the US Central Intelligent Agency (CIA) in the Middle East, and in 1975 Hezbe-Rastakhiz (the Resurgence Party) was established, and the Shah declared Iran a one-party state (Abrahamian 1982: 435–46; Halliday 1979: 64–103)

To summarise briefly, the process of economic development in the 1960s and 1970s was structurally and spatially uneven. The oil economy accumulated the surplus which financed industrialisation, the building of infrastructure and improved health, education and employment opportunities. The state bureaucracy provided some employment for a minority of urban women, while the majority of women constituted the bulk of semi-skilled, unskilled and unpaid family workers in industries where new technology was not applied and production remained labour-intensive. The female population remained smaller than the male population, which is characteristic of developing countries where women's health is neglected and their education lags behind that of men. Development marginalised the role of the clergy in the economy and society, although Sharia law determined gender roles and relations, as we shall see.

Gender and politics

A contradiction arose between modernisation and the persistence of Shii ideology in gender roles and relations. State-sponsored patriarchy perpetuated female subordination, despite the economic and political changes; nevertheless, women responded and struggled for change under the Shah's repressive regime.

The weakening of state power prior to the 1963 White Revolution allowed a degree of political struggle by women, workers, students and the clergy. In 1962 various women's organisations of the previous decade became active again. They campaigned vigorously for women's right to vote, by lobbying ministers and *Majles* deputies. Finally a law was drafted, but, under pressure from the clergy's opposition to the bill, its implementation was postponed. The women's campaign intensified, petitions were signed, letters were sent to politicians and the media. In January 1963 they refused to celebrate Reza Shah's women's day, the day of compulsory unveiling. Women teachers, civil servants and employees of private enterprises called for a day's general strike, marched to the prime minister's office and presented their demand. Finally on 27 February 1963 women won electoral rights (Hendessi 1990: 8; Sanasarian 1982: 82–3).

The White Revolution allowed the Shah to consolidate his power under American tutelage. The increase in oil revenue changed the character of the state, which no longer relied on taxation for revenue. This made the Shah's dictatorial state different from his father's. Under Reza Shah the political elite participated in decision making; under his son they were silenced. He saw himself not just as the head of state, but as its embodiment. Citizens were no longer expected to participate in state-building. He was building a state based on oil revenue, and the citizens were to serve it, benefit from it, and be obedient and grateful to him (Najmabadi 1991: 58–9).

Women's activities, therefore, were not only controlled by the state; they were initiated by the state. In a famous interview with Oriana Fallaci, the Shah rejected the whole notion of gender equality by expressing his contemptuous attitude to women. He asserted that 'you may be equal in the eyes of the law but not in ability, as you have never produced a Michelangelo, a Bach or even a good chef' (Fallaci 1976: 271–2). But under domestic and international pressure he made some reforms on behalf of women at times calculated to enhance his international image. In 1963 six women were elected as *Majles* deputies and two more were appointed by the Shah to the senate. In 1965 he appointed Faroukhru Parsa as the first female minister for education (Sanasarian 1982: 79–100).

In 1966 Shoraye Aliye Jamiate Zanan (High Council of Women's Association) was dissolved and replaced by Sazemaneh Zanan Iran

(Women's Organisation of Iran, WOI). Thirty-three associations (religious and national minorities, charities and some professional groups) constituted its structure and membership (Iran Almanac 1967: 518–25). Many active members of this organisation came from families who had been involved in the political struggles of the previous decades. They developed certain ideas for family law reforms but they had to wait until it suited the Shah to grant them. In the mid-1970s, for example, Manochehrian, a woman senator and lawyer, proposed that the requirement of the husband's permission for a married woman to obtain a passport be eliminated. Her proposal was rejected and she was forced to resign her seat (Najmabadi 1991: 63).

Nevertheless, the WOI created family welfare centres in various parts of the country. It provided health, education, legal aid, child-care facilities, vocational training and free contraception. In 1967 the Family Protection Act (FPA) reformed family law. According to this reform, a man could marry a second wife only with the permission of the court. In 1975 the consent of the first wife was added, unless she was unable to have sexual relations with her husband or unable to bear children. The first wife also had the right to seek divorce if her husband married a second wife. A woman could apply for divorce if her husband was unable to have sexual relations with her, was unable to provide for her, ill-treated her, suffered from contagious disease, abandoned her or was insane. Divorce could be obtained only in the civil courts. The 1975 Act also raised the age of marriage to 18 for women and 20 for men. In 1977 abortion was legalised, but married women had to obtain their husband's written consent. Unmarried women upon their written request could have an abortion.

These reforms were ambiguous. For example, consent to a husband's polygamy was often given because the woman feared her husband's violence. The reforms did not contradict *Sharia* law, but left women as inferior beings in many ways. Women could not be employed on the political staff of the foreign ministry; in the course of land reform, land was sold only to men. The man was still the head of the family: a wife was still legally forbidden to hold a job which the husband considered damaging to the dignity and prestige of the family; a woman could not leave the country without the permission of her husband or father; the wife was not free to choose her place of residence. A woman, regardless of her age, had to obtain her father's permission to marry for the first time; at divorce, the husband retained custody of the children – even with the husband's death, it was the husband's father who automatically became guardian of the children and not the children's mother. According to *ghesas* (the law of retribution), a part of *Sharia* law, it was not a criminal offence for a man to kill his wife for the defence of his dignity. The Muslim system of polygamy, under which a man can have four wives, remained legal, although the number of polygamous marriages declined for economic reasons and strengthened the nuclear family relationship. *Sighe* (temporary marriage), when a man takes a woman as his wife for a limited period, continued to be sanctioned by the Shii clergy (Bahar 1983: 182; Sanasarian 1982: 88–96).

The reform of the labour law was a step forward for female workers. For example, in the 1970s employers were responsible for a woman's maternity pay through the workers' insurance scheme. Paid maternity leave was ten weeks (six weeks before and four weeks after childbirth). All workplaces that had more than ten women with babies had to organise a nursery, and women were allowed to breast-feed every three hours. But many workplaces had no nursery and children had to be left with parents, friends and neighbours. Women (except nurses) were forbidden to work between 10 p.m. and 6 a.m., and to do heavy work, as they were considered weak. This was in accordance with Islamic ideology of giving priority to family structure and making women available for their families; it discriminated against women as they were categorised as unskilled and therefore low-paid (Pakizehgi 1978: 222–3).

Similarly, by 1975, the number of women in highly professional categories increased: eighteen female *Majles* deputies, two senators, two deputy ministers, twenty-eight court lawyers and a few hundred councillors. In 1975 the Shah ordered the WOI to join the Rastakhiz party, and selected five women to be on its executive board. But in summer 1978, when political opposition to the Shah escalated, he gave concessions to the religious leaders, who were asking for greater adherence to Islam by reversing women's rights. He reduced the age of marriage for girls from 18 to 15, and dropped the post of Minister of State for Women's Affairs. The incumbent, Mahnaz Afkhami, who was also the secretary-general of the WOI, was not given any other cabinet post (Sanasarian 1982: 100–114).

These reforms had been part of the culture of modernity that resulted from the development of capitalism in Iran, with its accompanying industrialisation and the establishment of new political and social institutions based on the western model. They barely affected the lives of the majority of rural women, who remained poor or unpaid, illiterate family workers. The majority of working-class women in urban areas constituted the first generation of rural migrants who lived in shanty towns, in poverty, with limited education and a subsistence wage. Both groups remained attached to Islamic values.

Thus the Shah's state, in the 1960s and 1970s, entitled only a minority of women to some reforms. Moreover, the *bazaar* economy and its associated traditional middle class were weakened. This meant that the role of those who carried out retail, export trade and manufacture of traditional commodities declined. The growth of supermarkets, department stores and large banks reduced the role of the *bazaar*. Instead, those who, with the help of the state, retailed, imported, exported and manufactured modern commodities, or those who participated in the state bureaucracy, became the dominant class, encouraged and supported by the state. The political power of the traditional middle class was also undermined by the weakening of the mosque. But the unevenness of economic development meant that their economic and political decline was relative. Massive migration from the rural areas made their existence viable as there was a need for petty retailers, *bazaar* wholesalers and money-lenders. Therefore their numbers remained considerable, and they became hostile to the Shah's reforms, as traditional *bazaar* values – the close family, financial and cultural ties with the *olama* – were being undermined by values associated with modernisation (Keddie 1981: 244–5).

The impact of this modernisation was particularly painful for traditional middle-class women. They had to endure modernisation observing the absolute Islamic values of segregation, including wearing the *chador*, dictated by their families, especially male relatives who regarded the culture of modernity as horrific and inap-

propriate for their women. For respecting these values and traditions,
on the other hand, they had to pay the heavy price of being labelled
as backward in schools, universities and workplaces. These women
were torn between their families' traditional values and a society
which promoted western values, including wearing the latest European fashions. They were expected by their families to leave home
wearing the chador as a sign of honouring tradition. But outside of
the home they felt rejected for wearing the chador, which was assumed to be a sign of backwardness. Many tried to resolve this
dilemma by accommodating both values. They left home veiled and
took their veil off before entering school, university or the workplace. But many others, under family pressure, took a defensive
position and wore the veil as a sign of protest at the uneven economic, political and social change (Tabari 1982: 9–10).

The impact of modernisation and secularisation on the modern
middle class was different. It allowed the development of new ideas,
and encouraged a degree of struggle to challenge patriarchal values.
Despite political repression and the continuation of traditional values
attached to Shii gender ideology, a small but nevertheless significant number of women experienced, to a limited extent, some
aspects of the women's liberation occurring in other parts of the
world. These women began to fight traditional values as a way of
freeing themselves from the double standard of male-centred values
and perceptions of how women should behave. They fought for
divorce and refused mahr and nafaghe, which are essential conditions
in an Islamic marriage. This rejection was a protest against the
treatment of women's sexuality and reproductive role as a tradable
commodity, against male entitlement to female services, and against
control over her sexuality, fertility and activities inside and outside
the home. These women began temporary or permanent relationships with men, including sexual relationships, outside marriage.
But their experience was no less painful than that of traditional
middle-class women, as this behaviour was unacceptable and un-
forgivable within the family and society. Families, regardless of
their secular or Islamic sympathies, began to reject gharbzadegi
('westoxication'), which meant celebration of the corrupt culture
of the west. A gharbzadeh woman, a woman who transgressed the
norm of her community, came under strong attack. The imposition

of social control, varying according to the degree of secular belief of the family, was a common thread throughout society in denouncing the *gharbzadeh* woman and limiting her moral influence (Najmabadi 1991: 64–5).

My own experience of this period was similar to that of many young women who were the victims of the contradictory rules of having secular education and being expected to participate in the public sphere, but at the same time bound to Islamic values of morality. My socialisation was totally secular and members of my family were supporters of the communist and nationalist movements in the 1950s, when close relatives were imprisoned and tortured. In the 1960s and 1970s, when these movements were suppressed, my family became sympathetic to modernisation. However, they pressurised me to get married when I was 17 and still at school. Their fear was that the culture of *gharbzadegi* would lead me to moral degeneration. Under these pressures I got married, hoping to be able to free myself from my family's double standard. My marriage survived only three years, during which time I had two children and did not feel free from male-centred values and perceptions. I resented all the forces that inhibited my potential and dared to break the norm by leaving my husband and demanding divorce. My punishment was to be denied not only the custody of my children, according to Islamic law, but also access to them.

Many women suffered another dual role expected of them by religion and the state. An Iranian woman I interviewed in London in 1992 explained how she was forced by her mother to undergo a virginity test, failure of which would render her unable to marry a man who was superior to her. Another, despite her secular education and style of life, was made so paranoid about her virginity that when she sat an entry examination for a teachers' training course, she wrote nothing on the answer sheet in order to fail, because part of the examination involved a virginity test, and she was scared by the idea that she might not be a virgin. These may be individual experiences but they represent those of many others (Poya 1992: 141–62).

My generation was greatly inspired by Forough Farokhzad (1935–67), a great feminist, poet and film-maker. She married at 16 and was 18 when her son was born. Two years later she left her husband, lost the custody of her child and was denied visits to him. She expressed her pain and grief in her poetry collections *Asir* (Captive) and *Divar* (Wall). She lived the free, varied life usually reserved for men. She dared to write about her sexuality, feelings and activities in her poetry. In her other collections, *Osian* (Rebellion), *Tavaledi Digar* (Another Birth) and *Iman Biavarim be Aghaze Fasle Sard* (Let Us Believe in the Dawn of the Cold Season), she expressed the feeling of many young women of that period who were the victims of the popular perception of the illegitimacy and immorality of contravening norms. In 1967, at the age of 32, she died in a car accident. She devoted her life and work to exposing the double standard of male-centred values and perceptions and how those values manipulated women and confused their lives, making them unable to operate within a patriarchal system. Her poetry expressed hostility towards a secular state and economy which preserved all the traditional values that hindered changing the unequal treatment of men and women (Milani 1985: 317–31; Keddie 1981: 196; Warnock Fernea and Qattan Bezirgan 1977: 291–319).

In the 1970s women's political participation both inside and outside the country increased. Many women during this period realised that as long as poverty and repression existed in Iran women would continue to be regarded as inferior beings. They played an important role in the fight against the system. Even the official statistics estimated that there were thousands of women political prisoners in the Shah's jails. While torture was a common fate for all political prisoners, women were subjected to particularly cruel and degrading forms of torture, including rape. Iranian women abroad joined the anti-Shah struggle, and were active for many years in student, political and women's organisations.

The secular opposition consisted of a number of small organisations, operating underground. The most important one was Cherikhaye Fedaiye Khalghe (Fedayeen Guerrilla Organisation), which developed out of a split from the pro-Soviet Tudeh party. They believed in armed struggle as the prime means of overthrowing the regime. They adopted a variant of Marxist dependency theory and borrowed an analysis and strategy of national liberation that called for popular unity of the masses against the regime and imperialism. Many women activists joined this organisation in Iran;

many were arrested, tortured or killed. Well known among them was Ashraf Dehghani, one of the founding and leading members of the organisation, who escaped from prison and in exile wrote her book Hemaseh Moghavemat (The Legend of Resistance) and revealed facts about the condition of political prisoners in Iran. She continued her struggle in exile and returned to Iran during the 1979 revolution (Bahar 1983: 184).

But within the secular left there was ignorance of and lack of interest in women's issues. Struggle against gender inequality was considered divisive, jeopardizing the unity of the movement. The task was to raise the slogan of equality and liberation of women, and wait until the victory of socialism. Disillusioned and isolated both on personal and on political levels, I joined the many other Iranian women abroad. I became involved in the women's and students' movement of the 1970s, but soon became known to SAVAK and had to remain in exile until the 1979 revolution.

The secular left as a whole was isolated. They failed to understand the contradictory changes taking place in Iran. They blindly followed their formulae for liberation and socialism, failing to relate to the majority of the population, who were affected by the contradictions of economic and socio-political development. They did not relate to class, gender and racial inequalities in society except in an abstract way, as was the case with religion and religious values. This facilitated the easy takeover of power by the conservative Islamic opposition.

The most important body on the Islamic opposition was Mujahedeen Khalgh (the Islamic Guerrilla organisation), which developed from the religious wing of the National Front, led by Ayatollah Taleghani, in the 1960s. They believed in a link between Islam and modern ideas (Abrahamian: 1982: 464–73; Keddie 1981: 236–9). Many women joined the Mujahedeen. Two women, Mother Rezai and Mother Shayegan, symbolised the resistance of Iranian mothers whose children were tortured and killed by SAVAK, but they remained in opposition and were themselves arrested and tortured (Bahar 1983: 183–4).

Ali Shariati, a French-educated sociologist inspired by Frantz Fanon, was the ideologue of modernised Islam.[2] His message was that Islam, particularly Shiism, was a revolutionary ideology that

permeated all spheres of life, especially politics, and inspired true
believers to fight against all forms of oppression, exploitation and
social injustice. Ayatollah Khomeini led the clerical opposition to
the Shah's regime from exile, first in Turkey and later in Iraq in the
1960s and 1970s. He opposed the regime for being a threat to Islam
and to nationalism in Iran. He did not attack the communists or
nationalists, nor comment upon women's rights issues. He attacked
the Shah's regime for exploiting the country's resources and the
people and for using women as sex objects to promote consumerism. He stated that in Islam women and men are equal (Abrahamian
1982: 450–80; Sanasarian 1982: 117).

In reality, Shariati's Islamic populism complemented Khomeini's
theory of *velayat faqih* (governance of the religious jurist). This meant
the Islamisation of the state and society on the model of the
original Islamic community of the prophet Muhammad and his
immediate successors. This fundamentalist Islam insists that Islam
is a religion and a state. An Islamic state must apply the tenets of
Islamic doctrine, above all *Sharia* law to all aspects of social and
economic life. So Ayatollah Khomeini was explicitly rejecting the
secular state. Throughout the 1970s he urged not only an adherence
to Islamic law but the establishment of an Islamic state (Bakhash
1985: 38–40; Rose 1983: 166–88). Shariati did not oppose this,
but he insisted that all modern concepts and doctrines of European
social thought are contained in a superior form in the Quran. The
opposition interpreted Shariati's writing and speeches as being
secular and believed that Ayatollah Khomeini was on their side
(Zubaida 1982).

Shariati died in 1977 and left Ayatollah Khomeini as the leader of
the opposition. In October 1978 Khomeini moved to Neuphle-le-
Chateau, near Paris. This strengthened him as he had access to
journalists from the world's leading media to express his views.
Iranian political leaders (National Front, Fedayeen, Mujahedeen and
the Tudeh party) visited Ayatollah Khomeini in his new headquarters and acknowledged his domination of the opposition movement. The groundwork was laid for the Islamic state.

In January 1979, as a journalist, I visited Ayatollah Khomeini in
Neuphle-le-Chateau. I was told that I had to wear a black *chador*,
otherwise he would not receive me. I explained to him that my

family and close relatives opposed the Shah's regime and suffered persecution and that I had also suffered personal and political repression. Thus, as a woman looking forward to an end to the dictatorial system of the Pahlavi, I was desperate to know whether women in Islamic Iran would be allowed higher education, to work equally alongside men in paid employment and have equal rights with men in the family and under the law. He did not answer my questions and practically asked me to leave by angrily saying that 'Yes, we have said it all. The problem is that you are talking too much, woman. Goodbye.'

The secular opposition and the traditional middle class cemented their alliance with Ayatollah Khomeini. The struggle in the streets and workplaces intensified. Khomeini's and Shariati's messages expressed the feelings and aspirations of the urban poor more effectively than the liberal and the left political groups who were attracted to Shariati's views. The majority of the population could not identify with the secular opposition, and preferred the religious opposition. Their lives were worlds away from those of the small minority who benefited from the process of economic development under the Pahlavi. The Islamic opposition took the form of nationalism in favour of independence from the Shah's repressive regime and its American ally.

Opposition to the Shah's regime escalated throughout 1978. Until June, the demonstrations were composed predominantly of intellectuals, students and the urban poor. From September, workers effectively shut down almost all industrial establishments and services. Among the first strikers were women in telecommunications, nurses and hospital workers. As the strikes spread, with oil workers playing the most important role by reducing production to the amount necessary for internal consumption, women teachers, civil servants and factory workers also participated intensively (Bahar 1983: 184–8; Abrahamian 1982: 496–525).

Finally, on 16 January 1979, after eighteen months of bitter struggle, the Shah was forced to leave the country. On 1 February Ayatollah Khomeini returned to Iran from exile in Paris. Five days later he declared himself head of state. The nationalist and communist organisations mistakenly regarded Khomeini's Islamic anti-imperialism and anti-capitalism as an advance towards nationalism and socialism. So they participated in the establishment of the Islamic state.

Conclusion

This chapter has shown how the interrelationship between capitalist development under foreign domination, Shii Islam ideology and class formation in twentieth-century Iran has produced uneven economic, social and political developments. The state, as the main agent of capital accumulation, determined and regulated social relations within production and reproduction, between classes and genders. It operated as one single system of capitalism and patriarchy and determined the way women should be incorporated into the public sphere.

Under the influence of the state, capital and religion, different social classes at different periods have had different access to material resources, different values attached to religious ideology and different degrees of political power. Whenever the power of the state weakened, women struggled and forced the state to reform. Reforms were made in relation to women's education, employment, unveiling and desegregation.

But this uneven development did not allow the majority of women to benefit from the changes. The majority of working women remained unpaid or low-paid. A minority benefited from secular education, reform of family law and opportunities in the labour market. Some even occupied important positions. Despite this, women's independence in the family and their independent presence in the public sphere were opposed. The state maintained its legitimacy by making concessions to Shii Islam gender ideology. Although the form of female subordination changed at different periods and affected different classes in different ways, gender identity based on Islamic tradition maintained sexual hierarchies, sexual division of labour and, as a result, female subordination.

Notes

1. This was the womens' organisation of the pro-Soviet communist Tudeh (Masses) party.

2. For an excellent analysis of Shariati's role see Rahnema 1998, 1994.

Chapter 3

The Islamic Sexual Division of Labour

Following the 1979 revolution, the Islamic state rejected the Shah's economic policy and advocated an Islamic command economy, isolated from the global economy. It expanded the state sector and intended to isolate the private sector. This policy, combined with an international trade ban on Iran, led to economic depression. During this period, the state, based on its principles of Islamic gender relations, also implemented policies aimed at the complete exclusion of women from the public sphere, especially employment. The Islamic defence of women's place in the home was that during the Pahlavi era a culture of consumerism was promoted which led to moral degeneration and the breakdown of Islamic values. The state, therefore, strengthened patriarchal relations in marriage and family life by undoing family law reforms. Motherhood and wifehood were considered the most important tasks for women, while breadwinning was the responsibility of men. The process of excluding women from the labour market was to begin with a policy of gender segregation in the public domain: strict dress codes for women and the introduction of gender division in education and employment, which inevitably resulted in many women losing their jobs.

Women in the Economy on the Eve of Revolution

Statistics published under the Shah in 1978 included the state ministries' employment in 1974/5: a total of 297,863, of whom 87,474 (29 per cent) were women (Iran Statistical Yearbook 1977/8: 66).

According to the Iranian national census, the state sector was that which employed workers in government or government-affiliated organisations for a wage or salary. Government-affiliated organisations were those in which at least half of the stock was government-owned. They operated under Ghanoone Estekhdame Keshvari (the country's employment law). The percentage of women workers was highest in the ministries of education (41 per cent), higher education (39 per cent), tourism (27 per cent), trade (27 per cent) and health (26 per cent).

Aside from the administrative sector, in 1972/3 there were 3,973 industrial enterprises in Iran employing more than ten workers, of which 97 per cent were owned and controlled by private entrepreneurs; 2 per cent were owned and controlled by the state and 1 per cent were joint ventures between the state and a private entrepreneur. They employed a total workforce of 249,649, of which 19,459 (8 per cent) were women (Iran Statistical Yearbook 1977/8: 383–7). Women were relatively concentrated in smaller industries categorised as 'others' (15 per cent), textiles (10 per cent), chemicals (11 per cent) and food (9 per cent).

There were also a large number of private enterprises employing fewer than ten people, divided into the following categories: employers (all persons who owned all or part of an establishment, and who had at least one employee), self-employed (all persons who owned all or part of an establishment but either worked alone or employed only unpaid family workers), private sector employees (who worked for a wage or salary), and unpaid family workers.

These enterprises operated under Ghanoone Kar va Omoreh Ejtemaie (the Labour Law and Social Affairs). In 1972/3 they employed 6,922,000 people, of whom 648,000 (9 per cent) were women (Iran Statistical Yearbook 1977/8: 50). Women constituted 17 per cent of unpaid family workers, 10 per cent of wage and salary earners, 7 per cent of the self-employed and 1 per cent of employers.

A Minimal Demand for Female Labour

After the revolution in 1979, Ayatollah Khomeini argued that the Shah and his regime had plundered the country's resources by over-spending and promoting western-oriented consumerism. He suggested that an Islamic economic system, based on self-sufficiency, would end all the plundering and usurpation of wealth (Rahnema and Nomani 1990: 235–7; Algar 1981: 115–16). Hence the political slogan 'Neither East, nor West, but Islamic Republic' became popular. The ideal Islamic economic system was seen as self-sufficient, agriculturally oriented small-scale production, with little or ideally no contact with the outside world's values, ideas, production relations or technology. It was claimed that under an Islamic economic system land, labour and capital would be utilised according to Sharia. This allotted landlords a fair rent, capitalists a fair profit and workers a fair wage. The ideal relationship between labour and capital was based on co-operation. Wage bargaining and trade unionism were considered unfair, and both capitalists and workers were prohibited from exploiting one another. Borrowing was to be interest-free, but despite this capital could grow, because Islam allows profit which acts as an incentive to save. Moreover, the institution of zakat (Islamic tax) would inhibit accumulation and concentration of capital in few hands. The Islamic state was entitled to hold considerable economic power: to own property, receive taxes, organise and dispose of state and public properties and revenues (Rahnema and Nomani 1990: 239–42).

This philosophy engendered policies which led to the confiscation of property belonging to the Pahlavi and their allies – private domestic owners of capital and their counterparts who had fled the country. Their property was brought under state ownership and control. Bonyade Mostasaffin (the Foundation for the Disadvantaged) was established to administer these properties, which included mining and manufacturing enterprises, commercial farms, construction companies, trading and other service enterprises. A large state bureaucracy was created to administer the Islamisation of society. The workers in this new social bureaucracy consisted of some of the traditional middle class, the urban poor and lumpen elements who provided an important support for Khomeini in the vital years after the fall of the Shah (Behdad 1995a: 99–103; Poya 1991).

There was no controversy among the Islamic leaders on the economic role of the state. There was a dispute, however, over the extent and the means by which the state should intervene in the operation of the private sector (Rahnema and Nomani 1990: 146–

59). Moreover, the enlarged state sector was heavily underfunded. A ban on Iranian oil imports had been adopted immediately after the US embassy occupation in November 1979 (see Chapter 6). This led to a fall in revenue, which diminished the state's capacity to invest and subsidise. Private entrepreneurs who remained in the country and continued their activities under the Islamic state also relied on state regulation and subsidies. Therefore all sectors of the economy suffered and the result was declining output and rising unemployment (Behdad 1995a: 103).

Iran's isolation also meant that the value of the Rial collapsed in the world market; in 1979 it fell from 70 Rials to 1,750 Rials to the US dollar. This situation undermined Iran's foreign trade and created shortages and inflation. Under pressure from the *shoras* (workers' councils – see Chapter 6) wages had increased. As a result of inflation, however, real wages fell and therefore the increases did not help many poorer families. Unemployment and inflation drastically reduced purchasing power (Poya: 1991: 96–9).

During this period the public behaviour of women became a central issue. The Shah's regime was denounced as decadent and the cause of corruption of womanhood. A liberated woman was declared to be one who followed the path of Fatimah, daughter of the prophet Mohammad, and Zaynab, her daughter. As previously explained, Fatimah represents and symbolises motherhood and womanhood, the perfect mother and wife in the sphere of the home, and Zaynab represents and symbolises the woman in the political and social sphere, fighting for Islam alongside men in the battlefields. A large number of women were sacked because they did not comply with Islamic dress and behaviour codes. Many others were offered early retirement and redundancy. Hence economic depression combined with the state's policy of women's place being in the home to reduce the demand for women's labour and increased impoverishment.

The explanation for sending women back to the home was that, like Zaynab, women had fulfilled their responsibilities in public political life through demonstrations to bring about the revolution and an Islamic society. Now that the Islamic state had been established, they had to go back to their main responsibility in the home and the family, acting 'like Fatimah'.

At the heart of this position was a belief in the biological and

psychological differences between the sexes expressed in the writings of prominent Shii clergy in Iran such as Majlesi, Motahhari,
Nouri and Tabatabai. Nouri (1964/5) and Tabatabai (1979/80) have
used this argument to exclude women from holding positions in
government, the assumption of the profession of judges, managerial
positions and participation in war. Majlesi (1979) has also used these
arguments to justify women's place in the home, allocating the
responsibility for breadwinning and protecting the family honour
to men. Motahhari (1981) discusses extensively the relationship
between gender differences and the question of men's responsibility
to maintain, protect and control women, children and the family.

Even Shariati, whose writings were considered progressive and
radical by liberal and left political groups, advocated the same
principle by suggesting that the ideal woman in an Islamic society
is Fatimah: 'As a mother she raised a daughter like Zaynab and sons
like Hosein and Hassan. In a different aspect she was an exemplary
wife, one that stayed every inch of the way with Ali through his
loneliness, difficulties, problems and great moments' (Shariati 1990/
1: 239). On this basis, Zahra Rahnavard, a writer on women's issues
known as a Muslim feminist, argued:

> Motherhood and wifehood is the road to freedom and liberation. A
> woman has the revolutionary responsibility of showing the right path
> and prohibiting the wrong deed, decrying the false and teaching the
> right. It is women who teach the future generations and it is women
> who must endorse or reject any political agenda. (Rahnavard n.d:
> 103–10)

As a result of this ideology the state either forbade employment or
made conditions increasingly difficult. Many women lost their jobs
in the legal profession. Many others were removed from top government posts. On 3 March 1979, a decree forbade women judges to
work since, according to Islam, women are not fit to judge. Only
those with the following characteristics can be judges: 'Male, adult,
Muslim, Shii, just, mojtahed (practising religious jurisprudence), legitimate child, with good and strong memory, able to write and read
and visualise' (Payame Hajar, 29 January 1992; Zanan, nos 4–6, 1993).
Following this, the ministry of justice refused to issue decrees con-
firming women judges (Ayandegan, March–July 1979), and qualified
women were told to apply for administrative posts in the judiciary.

On 6 March 1979, the Minister of Defence, General Madani, declared that women would not be drafted into the army in future. All women serving their conscription terms were dismissed and released from military service. On 9 June 1979, the swearing-in ceremony of new judges took place without the participation of women nominees. The minister of justice told the press that other posts would be given to women trained for judicial responsibilities. In October 1979, the cabinet ratified a decree officially transferring women judges and lawyers to legal departments in other ministries (Moghadam 1988: 226; Tabari and Yeganeh 1982: 235–6).

On 2 December 1979, the Constitution of the Islamic Republic of Iran was ratified. It declared that the Islamic foundation of the state would be derived from Khomeini's theory of *velayat fagih*. Under the heading 'Women and the Constitution' it stated:

> The family is the cornerstone of society and the primary institution for the growth and improvement of the individual; consensus and ideological belief in the principle that the formation of family is fundamental for the future development of the individual is one of the main aims of the Islamic government. (Nashat 1983: 207)

A variety of methods were used to discourage women from employment. A large number of women were sacked for not complying with *hejabe eslami* (Islamic dress). Azar, a 35-year-old teacher, explained:

> As Islamisation spread and was consolidated, things became more and more difficult. One could be dismissed for 'unIslamic' behaviour, that is for talking to male colleagues or wearing make-up. Finally, when wearing Islamic clothes became compulsory, a large number of women were sacked for being *bad hejabi* (not complying with Islamic dress).

Maryam, a teacher, also explained how women were pushed out of workplaces:

> The condition of work became very harsh. The staff rooms were segregated. If women talked to men, it was 'unIslamic' behaviour and enough to cause dismissal. Before Islamisation colleagues and friends used to organise *dooreh* (getting together socially) in the evenings or at the weekends. It was a cheap and enjoyable form of entertainment as well as catching up with the news about our profession, our job and condition of work. We had to stop these gatherings, in case the informers reported us to the authorities for 'unIslamic' behaviour. I am a religious woman;

even under the Shah I dressed and behaved modestly. These rules and regulations are not Islamic. Those who are in control are opportunist; they are corrupt and they do anything to become the new elite.

On 6 May 1980 the Islamic Republic Party declared that that day, Fatimah's birthday, was to be celebrated as Women's Day. This was to emphasise the Islamic character of the state and signify the virtues of motherhood as symbolised by Fatimah. Following this, more women lost their jobs (Tabari and Yeganeh 1982: 237).

The age of retirement for females was reduced from 50 to 45 and their years of service to make them eligible for retirement were reduced from thirty to twenty-five. Maryam explained:

> The retirement law changed. They offered early retirement. If women were 45 and had 25 years of service they could retire and take home 25 days' salary a month. Before, men and women had to have 30 years of service. I, alongside many women, applied for early retirement. The conditions of work were very hard.

On 22 July 1980, all co-educational schools were abolished. Teaching was segregated, women teachers assigned to girls' schools and men to boys' schools. The Islamists argued that male heads of department must replace female secretaries with male secretaries. Male nurses should look after male patients and male teachers should teach male students.

When I interviewed a number of nurses, I learned that although nursing was seen as 'naturally' a woman's job, it was never considered respectable. It was believed that relationships between male doctors and female nurses could lead to fesad (moral degeneration), for which women were responsible and blamed. Nursing required night-shift work and close contact between female nurses, male patients and male doctors, which was not respectable. After Islamisation, this ideology was used to segregate the nursing profession, and, as a result, many female nurses lost their jobs.

Patriarchal Relations in Marriage and Family Life

The state's policies on employment were reinforced by a strengthening of patriarchal relations in marriage and family life through laws and regulations based on a traditional interpretation of Sharia.

On 26 February 1979, a few days after the revolution, the attack on the gains of the revolution began with attacks on women's rights. The Family Protection Act, the Shah's minimal reform of women's rights, was suspended. Ayatollah Khomeini returned to men the exclusive right to divorce and permitted them to take four permanent and an unlimited number of temporary wives (sighe) without the first wife's permission. The institution of sighe is a contract made for a limited period, which could be an hour. There is no divorce; the transaction ends at the end of the period and the woman has to wait 45 days (eddeh) before entering another sexual relationship, in case of pregnancy (Haeri 1994, 1989). According to articles 941,077 and 1,113 of the Islamic constitution, the man has no obligation to maintain the temporary wife. Therefore there is no mahr, nor nafaghe, and she has no inheritance rights (Keyhan 11 and 24 December 1990). Conventionally, female virgins do not become sighe. A woman who becomes sighe is labelled as 'not a good woman'.

In April 1979, Ghale Shahre Noe (the Tehran prostitution quarter) was burned down by the Hezbollah (Partisans of God). Eight thousand women lived in the Ghale. Many of them burned to death and many became homeless. On 12 July 1979, three prostitutes were executed. This was following Khomeini's speech when he said, 'if you flog four prostitutes, prostitution will end'. Later in the year, Ghale Shahre Noe was officially closed down by the Kanone Hemayate Eslami (the Centre For Islamic Protection). It ordered all prostitutes to introduce themselves to Daftare Ezdevaje Bonyade Eslami (the Islamic Foundation Marriage Bureau), where the women were made to become sighe.

On 2 October 1979, the Islamic family legislation was ratified by the Council of Islamic Revolution and included: a husband's right to forbid his wife to take employment – a woman had to obtain permission from her male kin to work, to travel, to study and to change her place of residence; in case of divorce, a father's right to have custody of female children over 7 and male children over 2, which passes to his relatives in case of his death; banning contraceptives and abortion (Tabari and Yeganeh 1982: 236; Keyhan 7 March 1979).

On 2 December 1979, the Constitution of the Islamic Republic of Iran was ratified, stating women's contemporary position:

In the creation of Islamic social institutions, all elements of humanity that hitherto served the multifaceted foreign exploitation of our country are to regain their true identity and human rights. As a part of this process, it is only natural that women should benefit from a particularly large augmentation of their rights because of the greater oppression that they suffered under the despotic regime. The family is the fundamental unit of society and the major centre for the growth and advancement of humanity. Compatibility with respect to belief and ideal is the main consideration in the establishment of a family, for the family provides the primary basis for humanity's development and growth. It is the duty of Islamic government to provide the necessary facilities for the attainment of this goal. This view of the family unit delivers woman from being regarded as an object or as an instrument in the service of consumerism and exploitation. Not only does woman recover thereby her momentous and precious function of motherhood, rearing alert and active human beings, she also becomes the fellow struggler of man in all the different areas of life. Given the weighty responsibilities that woman thus assumes, she is accorded in Islam great value and nobility. (Constitution of the Islamic Republic of Iran 1991: 13)

In July 1981 the *ghesas* law (the Bill of Retribution) replaced the civil laws. This meant that women were denied the minimum protection offered by the civil law in cases of marriage, divorce, custody of children, freedom of movement, murder, adultery, lesbianism, abortion and many other issues. According to *ghesas* law, harsh sentences, such as lashes and stoning to death, were to be practised on women for violations ranging from not totally complying with the Islamic dress code through to adultery. To prove murder, only male testimony was to be accepted. If a woman was killed by her husband because of adultery, her murder was not considered a crime (Paidar 1997: 348–53; Afkhami and Friedl 1994: 180–89; Tabari and Yeganeh 1982: 94–8).

Initially the Islamic state encouraged temporary marriage; the rationale was to bring about Islamic morality and harmony. However, a combination of economic problems, together with men's easy access to divorce and temporary marriage, created chaos and disorder in family relations and in the wider society. *Zane Rouz* weekly women's magazine reported that despite the closing down of the prostitution quarters, neither prostitution nor adultery had been eradicated. It also reported that under these circumstances women had become the victims of differential treatment by the law. It demonstrated that a larger percentage of women than men were sentenced to death because of prostitution. Many of them were forced into prostitution because of poverty. Many of these women were accused of adultery and were therefore executed. This was because adultery was proven on the basis of men's testimony, and women's testimony alone did not disprove adultery. In cases where four men testified women were sentenced to death (*Zane Rouz* 12 July 1980).

The chaos worsened further when physically and psychologically disabled men began to return from the war fronts. Women were encouraged to marry these men. Ayatollah Khomeini suggested that 'Those sisters who have lost their husbands in the war must re-marry with the disabled from the war in order to share their pain and bring more children to society' (*Zane Rouz* 12 June 1981). Mrs Behrouzi, a member of the *Majles*, argued that 'Marriage is a way to overcome many problems such as *zena* (adultery), poverty and pros-titution' (*Zane Rouz* 12 June 1981).[1]

Gender Segregation in Sports, Education and Public Places

On 9 March 1979, women were barred from sports on the grounds that coaches, judges and spectators in such events included men. On 8 July 1979, several Caspian Sea resort towns initiated a sexual segregation of the sea. Many women were flogged in public during the summer of 1979 on charges of swimming in the men's section. (Tabari and Yeganeh 1982: 233; *Ayandegan* 31 January 1979)

In the education system, gender segregation affected women even more adversely. The Islamic state's policy of excluding women from certain fields of study and areas of specialisation was to reinforce the ideology of women's place being in the home and to control the supply of female labour. On 21 May 1979, the ministry of education banned co-education. Educational institutions were ordered to seg-regate all classes. Many indicated that since the number of female students would not justify setting up separate classes, they would be unable to register any female students. In late September 1979, when schools opened, female students of technical training schools staged a protest against this decision. They were told to change their courses of training to fields where there were enough female students to justify separate courses (Tabari and Yeganeh 1982: 235).

On 3 June 1979, the Ministry of Education banned married women from attending ordinary high schools. They were told they should continue studies on their own and take part in special examinations in order to obtain degrees. With the lowering of the minimum age of marriage for women to 13, this meant a lowering of educational levels for women (Tabari and Yeganeh 1982: 235).

In Iran, demand for higher education has always been much greater than the supply of places. To enter these institutions students have to pass Konkour, a highly competitive entrance examination. In the first post-revolution nationwide entrance examination, in the academic year 1979–80, women were not admitted to degree courses in mining, Islamic jurisprudence, foundations of Islamic law, Islamic culture and Iranian civilisation. At the same time nursing schools admitted only single women (Mojab 1987: 4–5).

Gender segregation of the education system had a particularly negative effect on female education in rural areas. Azar, a school teacher and one of my respondents, explained:

> In the 1970s mixed schools opened and it became acceptable that boys and girls go to school together. In most rural areas there was only one school in a whole village. Because mixed schools were accepted by the rural population, girls were sent to the mixed school. But since Islamisation, girls' education has suffered. Because where there is only one school in a whole village only boys are given the chance.

According to the Islamic tenet advocated by scholars and the state, women were biologically and psychologically different from men. Therefore women and men had to be prepared for life differently. Article 30 of the Constitution of the Islamic Republic of Iran stated that the government was committed to providing free education for all, but Article 21 emphasised that women's rights to free education would be assured in conformity with Islamic criteria (Algar 1980; Higgins and Shoar-Ghaffari 1994). The basic goal of female education was the reproduction and stability of family relationships based on Islamic rights and morality, rather than the preparation of women for employment (Mehran 1989; Mohsenpour 1988).

As a result women were excluded from studying in many institutions. Either priority was given to male students or many courses were identified as unsuitable for women. In April 1980, Ayatollah Khomeini decreed Enghelabe Farhangi Eslami (Islamic Cultural

Revolution). The aim was to purge the universities of all opposition to the process of Islamisation, from left or right, and to give total political power to the Islamic societies which replaced student organisations. Following an armed attack on university campuses, injuring many students, all higher education institutions closed down (Mojab 1987: 6).

Segregating women and men in public places had not been anything like as successful. For example, to allocate certain rooms to men and certain rooms to women in workplaces had not been possible. To implement this policy successfully, new buildings would have had to be built to create more space. Nevertheless, in some cases women themselves had initiated segregation in workplaces precisely because it created space for them. Fataneh, a bank clerk, explained:

> In our workplace the management did not insist on segregating women and men into different rooms. But women prefer to work in a room without men, as they feel free and more comfortable to move around. For this reason we organise the rooms in a way that men and women are segregated.

Similarly, segregation on the buses had not been totally successful. On 30 July 1980, the Tehran Bus Company announced that the first three rows of seats in buses would be allocated to women (Tabari and Yeganeh 1982: 238). Later most buses specified such a section at the back of the buses. The proportion was one-third of seats for women and two-thirds for men. This corresponded with the official size of the male and female workforce, but in the rush hours the iron barriers in the middle of the buses were removed on many busy lines because women had the responsibility of taking their children to nursery school, or to their families and friends, before going to work. But generally women had welcomed segregation on the buses. Fatemah, a school teacher, said, 'Many women prefer the segregation on the buses; we feel more comfortable, as we are not sexually harassed by men.'

So the state on the whole succeeded in this period in segregating the sexes in sports grounds, in the education system and in public places. Women's responses varied. The majority of women did not object to segregation in public places, even if they had to sit separate from their husbands, as this had reduced sexual harassment and allowed women to participate in the public sphere without their families' objection. Women's objection to segregation in sports and education led to a change in the state's position (Ssee Chapter 5).

Islamic Dress: An Effective Gender Segregation

In July 1980, after several months of bitter struggle by secular women in urban areas against Islamic dress, the wearing of *hejab eslami* became compulsory (see Chapter 6). The uniform consisted of wearing a *roposh* (a long dress with long sleeves), a pair of trousers underneath, thick socks, tights or stockings, and a *maghnae* (a very large scarf covering head, all hair and shoulders). At work this uniform had to be either black, grey or dark brown. To comply with the religious tenets a woman's whole body should be covered, except the face and hands.

Petitions were circulated in several government ministries asking women employees voluntarily to add their signatures to a statement supporting Islamic dress. Those who did not comply were sacked. Women television broadcasters who refused were replaced with women wearing full Islamic dress. Shops were ordered to refuse to sell goods to women not wearing Islamic dress. The media began an ideological war on women not complying, accusing them of being communist or capitalist (Poya 1992, 1987: 153; Tabari and Yeganeh 1982: 233).

Soon there were new security units: Sarollah (the Blood of God), Ershad Eslami (Islamic Guidance), Komiteh (local Islamic councils) and Pasdaran (the Revolutionary Guards). They patrolled the cities, hunting for the opposition and for women without *hejab*. No woman dared to appear in public without Islamic dress because so many women had bones broken and faces burned with acid. A woman whose scarf did not completely covered her forehead was stopped by a male Komiteh member, who pulled her scarf down and pushed a drawing pin into her forehead to hold it there.

Despite mass struggle by women in 1979–81 against the compulsory *hejab*, most had accepted it and some had welcomed it. Women who identified themselves as middle class and relatively secular objected to it, but because they were a minority they had been limited to a modification of the uniform. Because they had greater access to money and less ideological constraint, they were able to wear a modified version of the dress, sometimes compatible with the latest international fashion in terms of shape and colour. At work, however, they had to comply with the uniform. When I interviewed a number of these women, I was surprised to hear even from them that, although they objected to it, they found it more comfortable as it had reduced the degree of sexism. Zohreh, the manager of a chemical laboratory explained:

> I do not like to wear the *hejabe eslami*. It is ugly and I feel that women have to cover their body because men cannot help themselves to be sexist, sexually harass women and look at women as a sex object. But I have no choice than to accept that this is an unfortunate reality of our society. Exactly for this reason now that I am covered head to toe at work my expertise is appreciated much more than under the previous system. Now they look at me as a scientist while before they looked at me as a sex object.

The policy of *hejabe eslami* did not affect rural women nor those of different nationalities. They had continued to wear their national dress at home and at work, which is usually family-centred. As always, even under the Pahlavi, they only wore the *hejab* at public gatherings, especially when they received guests. They had, therefore, welcomed this policy, as they identify with the practice. Women who identified themselves as middle class or working class with a high level of religious observance had welcomed the uniform. This was despite their differences in terms of the amount of money they may spend on a more or less sophisticated form of the uniform. Islamic dress had given them the identity of 'good woman', advocated by the Islamic tenets and enforced by their own socialisation.

As discussed in Chapter 2, a culture of modernity under the Pahlavi had regarded women who wore Islamic dress as backward. These religious women were prohibited from working by male members of their families who did not regard modernity as appropriate for their women. Under the Islamic state, these women found gender segregation to their benefit, allowing some of them more opportunity to enter paid employment. Maryam explained:

> I like to wear the *hejabe eslami*. I feel that this is respecting the views of people like me. Under the previous regime, I could not get a job as a

nurse because I was wearing the *chador*. In 1976 one hospital, Sevomeh Shaaban, was set up by the Islamic *bazaaris* (Islamic traders from the bazaar). This was the only hospital which employed women like me.

In many cases *hejabe eslami* became a source of power for religious women. Many were employed by Islamic security organisations to ensure the full implementation of the practice. They became agents of the state in implementing social control, and this was approved by their male kin. This was empowering for them. They used their power against secular women by supporting the patriarchal rules and roles for women. They supported the state which created these measures for their empowerment. Mana, one of my respondents, explained:

> Many times I was arrested in the streets for not fully complying with compulsory *hejab*. I was always asked similar questions by female members of the Islamic security forces: 'Sister, how could your heart allow you to let the eyes of a *namahram* (strange) man look at your body? How could you make him guilty of sin?' I was dying to ask her: 'Sister why in your eyes am I guilty of his sin? Why is it that I am not only sinful for not being ashamed of my own body, but also guilty because a man harasses me by looking at me as a sex object? Why am I responsible for his faults, and why is it me who is driving a pure man to sin? Why do you see your value and your power in what you do for men, and for this you deny your own body and your visible presence?' I couldn't, though. If I had, I would have ended up in jail. (Poya 1992)

Conclusion

In this chapter I have shown how the state's initial gender and employment policy aimed at excluding women from the labour force in the first phase of Islamisation (1979–81). My field research demonstrated that the effect of the ideology of women's place being in the home, combined with economic depression and changes in laws, regulations, customs, policies and practices, reduced the demand for female labour. The Islamic state further strengthened patriarchal relations by creating separate spheres for women in the public domain, which ensured that women's reproductive role within the family was more important than their role in the public sphere, especially in employment. In this short period the impact of Islamic gender ideology was overwhelming. But the development of secular and religious responses to state Islamisation was diverse. This diversity, combined with the impact of economic circumstances of the war years, soon changed the position of the theocratic state on women's employment.

Note

1. Arranged marriages with soldiers continued, but did not seem to resolve the social problems. As late as 1987 a series of articles in the newspaper *Ettellaat* continued to encourage this form of marriage 'as a way to combat moral degeneration'. But the same articles pointed out that 'the economic problems of inflation, male unemployment and high rate of *mahr* had decreased the number of marriages' (*Ettellaat* 15–17 December 1987). To help this desperate situation Janbazan (the Freedom Fighters) was set up, and the *Majles* ratified Article 20 of the law, which allocated 1 billion Rials to this organisation to arrange and encourage marriage for the soldiers. In 1990 this fund increased to 2.5 billion Rials (*Keyhan* 14 November 1990).

Chapter 4

The Impact of the Iran–Iraq War

Following the beginning of the Iran–Iraq war the Islamic state's economic and gender and employment policies changed. The state had to respond to pressures of war, economic dislocations and rigidities in the labour market. Using interviews and statistical data, I have examined the factors which determined the demand of the state and private employers for female labour. In this period, the policy of sex segregation began to adapt. The Islamic state maintained its ideological stance, yet at the same time accommodated new economic circumstances. Although the ideological constraint placed women in a disadvantageous position within the labour market, paradoxically gender segregation opened up opportunities for religious women to enter employment, and even occupy important positions, for the first time. At the same time, the imposition of social control by the state (and men), and also women's own internalised control, posed major obstacles to the upward mobility of many female workers. The role of the war was not limited to its effect on the supply of and demand for female labour; it raised ideological issues concerning the very legitimacy of the state's hegemony. These interacted with people's material circumstances and provided the ground for changing the position of women in society.

Demand for Female Labour in the State Sector

Despite the effect of Islamic gender ideology, a number of factors soon increased the state's demand for female labour. The Iran–Iraq war (1980–89) reduced the supply of male labour; inflation was another factor, as was Iran's isolation in the world market. The war and the war economy increased the supply of women seeking work or resisting exclusion. The rigidities in the system, determined by the ideology of a gendered division of labour, generated continuing particular demands for female labour. Men were neither trained nor ideologically willing to do 'women's jobs', such as nursing, teaching, or secretarial and administrative work.

In this period, the state gradually changed its policy of self-sufficiency and its attempt to operate in isolation from a world economy dominated by the west, while continuing the slogan of 'neither East, nor West'. Iran, western and eastern countries all maintained their political rhetoric against each other, but at the same time Iran's oil was purchased and arms were sold to Iran by the back door. Therefore, there was a return to import-substitution industrialisation. However, the terms of trade moved against Iran. The Islamic state began to pay for imports through barter deals. Cheap oil was sold in return for expensive imports. The priority was given to food and military equipment. All this resulted in hoarding, shortages and a ration system, and consequently high inflation, officially recorded at 30 per cent in the 1980s (Behdad 1995b; Pesaran 1995; Poya 1991).

During this period, Islamic ideology concerning female participation outside the home also changed. Women were now mobilised by the state to cook, sew and prepare medicines, in the mosques, for men at the war fronts, acting as Zaynab. As a result, the demand for the unpaid labour of women increased and the state benefited from it economically and politically. Basseej Khaharan (the women's organisation for the mobilisation of irregulars for the war), one of many Islamic state organisations, had the responsibility for recruiting large numbers of women. The sons, husbands and fathers of many of these women were fighting. During this period, the organisation was financed by supporters' donations. It mobilised women in mass street demonstrations, and to work in the mosques for the men at the front. These women were called Khaharane Zaynab (Zaynab's Sisters), and their recruitment continued throughout the war years. There are no statistics to show the number of these women, but as late as winter 1988 a daily newspaper reported that,

Basseej Khaharan had a number of tasks: military and ideological training of women; helping the families of the Martyred and the families of
the prisoners of the war; to serve in the literacy corps; to teach in poor
rural areas voluntarily. Their main task, however, was to prepare medicines, repair the soldiers' clothes and prepare food for the soldiers in
the front lines. (Ettellaat 30 November 1988)

Even under these circumstances, where the state mobilised women
to be active outside the home, the emphasis was on the home being
women's priority. In an interview with a member of Basseej, one of
the women argued that 'although I am married and have children,
my activities have no adverse effect on my duties at home' (Basseej
Khaharan 30 November 1988). Elsewhere, Jebheh Ettellaat (the supplement
to Ettellaat daily newspaper) reminded women that 'in Islam it is not
necessary for women to go to war. Obeying the husband is equal
to becoming a mujahedeen [warrior for God]' (Jebhe Ettellaat 25 September
1989).

Unlike the previous period, when women were forced out of jobs,
they were now encouraged to work part-time. Zahra Rahnavard, a
state spokesperson on women's issues and known as a Muslim feminist writer, condemned the Shah's regime for encouraging female
employment that led to women's independence and the weakening
of family unity, which was against Islamic principles. Keyhan national
daily newspaper of 5 August 1981 reported her views:

Women under the previous system entered employment for a number
of reasons: the hatred of family life; to be independent; to help the
family's budget as the man's earnings were not enough; a few because
of their specialisation, but generally insecurity in relation to the family.
The Shah's objective was therefore to disrupt family life, to increase
bureaucracy, to create sexual chaos, and generally to create pro-western
family life.

Instead she put forward an alternative situation for the ideal Muslim
woman:

Men are responsible for nafagheh, therefore they must maintain the family.
Women's priority is to bring up children and perform domestic duties.
Only under certain circumstances could women go out to work: if their
domestic duties are not neglected and if this work is to promote Islamic
values. Under present economic difficulties, where women are forced to
go out to work, the government must promote men's employment

enabling them to maintain their families. Women's hours of work must be reduced to allow them to perform their domestic duties satisfactorily. Women who have specialisation and are financially secure must give up part of their earnings to help the economic problems of the country.

These arguments were not only ideological in terms of an Islamic philosophy that women's place is in the home to serve men and the family; they also reinforced gender subordination for the benefit of the state. Employing women part-time, paying women half a salary and reducing the hours of nursery schools saved government expenditure. *Zane Rouz* weekly women's magazine also suggested that women who had children could return to part-time work if their children were 3 years of age. This way the state nurseries would operate half of the time and women could look after their children the other half (*Zane Rouz* 14 May 1982).

Two years later in March 1984, Ayatollah Khomeini announced that: 'Women can participate in economic, political and social affairs within the Islamic laws and regulations' (*Ettellaat* 31 March 1984). This was a breakthrough. The economic pressure and the war were so hard on families that the state had to compromise its original position. However, this reconciliation needed Khomeini's approval. His speech legitimised women's work outside the home, as did a later speech of President Rafsanjani, but argued that the management of their money and property had to be supervised by men: 'Women, after performing their main responsibility of domestic work, could be involved in all levels of economic, social and political affairs. But, in Islam, because of the principle of *mahr* and *nafaghe*, women are not responsible for the breadwinning of the family' (*Ettellaat* 25 April 1984). Thus, during this period, the demand for female labour increased and was legitimised by the state. But the emphasis remained on part-time work, which reduced women's opportunity, ability and willingness to be in full-time employment with full-time entitlement. In April 1985 the *Majles* passed a law about women's part-time work. It was defined as half of full-time work, receiving half the salary, without any subsidies or entitlements. The minimum period of work was one year. Women could contribute to their pension at the full-time rate. They also had the same rights to maternity leave as full-time workers, but received only part-time pay (*Ettellaat* 8 April 1985).

The Islamic state inherited the Pahlavi structure of the public sector of the economy. The difference was that some state ministries closed down (Tourism, Rural Development and Art and Culture), and new ministries were formed (Plan and Budget, Accounting, Industries, Heavy Industries, Oil, and Radio–Television). Many Islamic institutions were also formed, some of which became ministries: Pasdaran (the Revolutionary Guards), Jihad (Reconstruction Crusades) and Ershade Eslami (Islamic Guidance). Other Islamic organisations also operated under state supervision: the Komitehs (local Islamic councils); Basseej (mobilisation of irregulars for the war) and Islamic societies (Anjomane Eslami), which replaced the shoras (workers' councils: see Chapter 6). These ministries and state organisations employed a large number of both male and female workers.

According to official statistics, by 1986/7, 54,388 men and 579 women were employed in the Reconstruction Crusade, and 7,083 men and 1,420 women were employed in Islamic Guidance organisations. Many more were employed in Pasdaran, Komiteh, Baseej and Islamic societies, for which there are no figures available. In 1986/7 state ministries employed 1,433,966, of which 1,014,422 were men and 419,544 were women. Thus, comparing the figures between 1986/7 and the pre-revolution situation (discussed in Chapter 3) the proportion of female workers (29 per cent) in different ministries did not change. In some ministries the percentage of women fell whilst in others it increased. For example, women in the ministry of education increased from 41 per cent to 43 per cent; in the ministry of health from 26 per cent to 41 per cent. In the ministry of higher education their share fell from 39 per cent to 19 per cent, and in the ministry of trade from 27 to 8 per cent. The ministry of tourism with its female workforce of 27 per cent closed down, but the female workforce of the ministry of Islamic guidance reached 17 per cent (Iran Statistical Yearbook 1986/7: 86).

The demand for female teachers and nurses increased, despite the initial attempt to stop women tending to male patients and teaching male students. Also, a significant number of women were employed in secretarial and administrative tasks. I interviewed a number of these women. They all pointed out that the demand for male nurses, secretaries and teachers increased; many men were trained and employed in these professions, but there was still a severe shortage mainly because these professions were seen as women's jobs. Maryam, a 35-year-old nurse, explained: 'Initially during the early years of the war, the injured Islamic soldiers objected to being treated by female nurses. Later, however, they had no choice as there was a real shortage of nurses and very few men wanted to become nurses.' The state, therefore, had to intervene and appeal to the soldiers to accept female nurses. In a series of articles, *Ettellaat* reported that, according to the international standard, for every 1,000 persons there had to be at least 3 nurses. Iran therefore should have had at least 120,000 nurses; in fact there were only 7,100. The articles also discussed the importance of female nurses and how they should be respected (*Ettellaat* 16–19 January 1986).

Similarly many female teachers returned to work, as sex segregation exacerbated the shortage of teachers. Maryam explained:

> Under the Shah's regime, male and female teachers taught at both single-sex and mixed schools. After the revolution, all schools became single-sex. Male teachers were to teach at boys' schools and female teachers at girls' schools. The result was that many girls' schools were left with very few teachers. So they allowed female and male teachers to teach at all primary schools but not at secondary schools.

The demand for women to re-enter administrative and secretarial work also continued. Although men were also encouraged to enter these jobs, they were traditionally categorised as women's jobs. Shahnaz, a 44-year-old head of a university department, explained: 'To employ male secretaries for male heads of departments and managers did not work out. Male secretaries were not as good as female secretaries. So female secretaries returned to work.'

By the mid-1980s, state ministries employed a large number of women. Islamic organisations increasingly employed women to deal with women's affairs. In education, health and administrative work the demand for female labour increased because of the inability or unwillingness of men to do 'women's' jobs. Nevertheless, the Islamic state still emphasised women's place in the home and part-time work outside the home, and in this way reinforced its stated gender ideology. Moreover, the state saved expenditure by entitling women to half a wage and not providing child-care facilities.

Demand for Female Labour in the Private Sector

The domestic crisis and the war with Iraq put pressure on Islamic statism and the command economy. By the mid-1980s the faction within the regime in favour of state intervention weakened, and the faction in favour of limiting it gradually took power. On the basis of *Sharia*, private property was revalued and the state encouraged the entrepreneur to invest and operate free from regulations and restrictions (Poya 1991: 96–9).

In the first phase of Islamisation, despite significant nationalisation, lack of investment by the private entrepreneur and lack of state subsidies in privately owned and controlled enterprises, private ownership of land and capital prevailed. Under the Islamic state the structure of the private sector remained the same as under the Pahlavi. In 1986/7 small private enterprises employed 7,119,000 workers, of whom 6,610,000 were men and 509,000 women (Iran Statistical Yearbook 1993: 69) In 1972/3, these enterprises had employed 6,922,000 workers, of whom 6,118,000 were men and 648,000 women. Despite an increase in the total number of workers, the percentage of women in different categories fell from 9 per cent to 7 per cent (see Chapter 3). For unpaid family workers, women's share increased from 17 per cent to 43 per cent (the majority being carpet-weavers and agricultural workers in household-centred workshops in rural areas); women as wage- and salary-earners fell from 10 per cent to 5 per cent; as self-employed from 7 per cent to 4 per cent, but as employers their share rose from 1 per cent to 4 per cent. Of these, the majority worked in urban areas (Iran Statistical Yearbook 1977/8: 50).

These statistics should be useful tools to indicate where women are in the labour market, but field research casts doubt on them. In rural areas many more women are carpet-weavers, cloth-weavers and agricultural workers than the statistics suggest, unpaid family workers invisible in the statistics. The product of their labour is sold by the men of their families in the market. Golrang, a carpet-weaver and agricultural worker, explained:

> I have been a carpet-weaver and an agricultural worker since I was seven years of age. I help my father in animal husbandry and my mother in agricultural work and carpet-weaving. Women do not get paid. In a

good year, when my father returns from selling the goods in the market, he gives my mother a sack or two of rice to sell within the village. With this money my mother buys gold, silver, household materials and appliances for me and my sister's *jahizieh* (trousseau). Similarly for carpet-weaving; my father sells the carpets in the market or sometimes he gives my mother a carpet to sell in the neighbourhood and she spends the money for me.

A large number of women in rural areas are not rewarded fully as wage labourers and do not appear in the statistics. The Islamic state has not intervened in these working conditions precisely because the work is unpaid and within the home.

Likewise, many women in the cities, self-employed and petty commodity producers or sellers, do not appear in the statistics, although their contribution is essential for the well-being of their families. I interviewed a group of ten self-employed women in a variety of jobs. Fataneh makes 'handbags, blankets and sheets and I sell them to the co-operatives. Sometimes I manage to sell 5–10 of each every day. This way I have been able to pay off all our debts.' Maryam makes 'pickles, jam, tomato puree and dried herbs and I sell them to the neighbours and to the shops in the area. This way I feed the family.' Pari makes 'decorative combs and hair clips. This helps us to keep going.' Pouran explained:

> One day as I was driving, I saw two women in the neighbourhood waiting for a taxi. I offered them a lift. They insisted on paying me. From then, I discussed this with women in the neighbourhood and asked them to use me as a taxi-driver. They agreed. I became a lady cab. I also work as a taxi-driver for the local nursery school. Without my earnings it would be impossible to survive the inflation.

Zari buys 'blank T-shirts, then I imprint on them and sell them to the co-operatives. This way I have been able to help with the mortgage.' Badri says: 'I grow plants and sell them door to door and to the co-operatives.'

They explained that their husbands' earnings were not enough to feed the family. They therefore had to take the initiative of producing goods at home and selling them door to door or to the co-operative chain stores. Although they recognised that their earning was important for their families, they did not categorise themselves as self-employed workers. Furthermore, no one ever asked them what they did, and they thought that if they were asked for statistical purposes, they would still call themselves housewife, because they produced the commodities while they were doing the housework. They and many women in the neighbourhood were also involved in buying rationed food cheaply and selling it on the black market, which could be categorised as self-employment. This, of course, did not appear in the statistics.

In urban and rural areas there is also a large number of women working for small private firms. By not registering these workers the employers escape paying tax to the state and benefits and insurance to the workers, and so they do not appear in the statistics. In the mid-1980s, the demand from these industries for female workers increased. This increase was dictated by the cheapness, flexibility and disposability of the female workforce, but hidden as a response to state labour laws.

According to the law, employers had to register their workers by contributing the equivalent of 20 per cent of each worker's salary for registration and insurance. Once the workers were registered, 7 per cent of their wage or salary was deducted as their insurance contribution. If employers did not contribute to their insurance, the workers could not be registered and no national insurance was paid. Holidays, sickness benefits, maternity benefits, insurance, tax allowances, pension and retirement were paid only to workers who were registered (the Labour Law 1981/2: 277–375).

There were men and women who worked unregistered for private enterprises. They were paid below the national minimum wage and received no benefits or subsidies. Many firms preferred to employ women because they could be hired and fired easily, and many women passed through these firms because this was the only way that they could get a job for a short working day. Women with children were particularly at the mercy of these employers because they often had to arrive late, leave early or bring their children to work because of the shortage of nursery schools. In the late 1980s and 1990s, the increase in the population of children under 10 also created shortages of schools and teachers. A shift system was introduced at schools. Tahereh explained how this made women's employment more problematic, and allowed private enterprises to exploit women workers more than ever before:

For four years I worked in a private medical clinic from 7 a.m. to 2 p.m. I had no break, I was paid half of the national minimum wage. The employer did not pay insurance for me or other workers. Therefore we received no benefits because we were not even registered anywhere as workers. We could see with our own eyes how the employer bribed the government agents in order to get away from paying tax and insurance. When my son was under 7 years of age [school age] my mother-in-law looked after him, because in these firms there were no workplace nurseries; state nurseries gave priority to state sector workers and I could not afford a private nursery's fees. When my son was 7 he went to school, morning shift only, 7.30–11.30. He then came to my workplace, stayed with me until I finished work at 2 p.m. Because of this they made me work overtime and during holidays without pay, to compensate for the hours that my son was there. Finally, when I complained to the Ministry of Labour, the attitude was that I should have known my rights better.

Lily had a similar experience:

I worked in a private company for 2 years. They would not pay insurance, although they paid the agreed minimum wage. When my first son was born I left the job for a year to look after him. When he was 1 year old, I left him with my mother-in-law and went back to work as a receptionist in a private clinic for two years. Again they paid no insurance for me. So for four years, although I was paid the minimum wage, I was not registered as a worker and lost all benefits and years of service. My second son was born, I left my job for another year and I returned to work when he was 1 year old. I got a job in a paint-making firm as a secretary. I demanded that they should register me and pay insurance for me. After a while they agreed and as a result I was registered as part of the workforce and received all the benefits. But going to work with two children was very difficult. At lunchtime I had to bring my older son to work until 2 p.m. As a result they made me work unpaid overtime and I lost many days of my paid holidays in order to pay back the hours that I went to collect my son and brought him to work for two hours every day.

Throughout the 1980s the number of female workers in these firms increased. For example, the government instructed shops selling women's clothes to employ female shop assistants only. A majority of these shops did not register their workers. When the law caught up with them, they sacked the women and employed new ones. These examples illustrate that a large number of women in urban areas were also invisible in the workforce statistics, while their contribution was essential for their families and for the national economy.

Gender ideology places these women workers at a disadvantage by undercounting and undervaluing their work. According to the labour laws the minimum wage in the mid-1980s was 45,000 Rials a month. Workers categorised as hourly paid, daily paid, seasonal workers or contract workers (those employed for one year at a time) received only the minimum wage, without any benefits or subsidies. The benefits and subsidies were extremely important and they made a great deal of difference in the final calculation of what the worker took home. For example the salary of a registered full-time worker included 45,000 Rials fixed minimum wage plus child benefit (calculated on the basis of three days' salary per month), housing benefit, food and cash bonuses and subsidies. These workers were also entitled to paid holidays and sickness benefits (Labour Law 1981/2). However, as discussed above, the majority of female workers did not receive these benefits because they were not registered.

Women's Preference for Work in the State Sector

Job security has made the state sector of the economy more attractive to both men and women seeking jobs than the private sector, despite lower wages. (Banks, whether state-owned or privately owned, had similar employment conditions and special advantages. For example, they offered favourable mortgage schemes to their employees; on the death of an employee, the loan would be cancelled and the property transferred to the inheritors.) However, women's preference for work in the state sector was determined by gender ideology, enforced by the state's policy and practice. State workplaces were physically large, and sexual segregation and social control could be implemented easily in order to avoid fesad (moral degeneration). Women were regarded as both corrupting and corruptible. The concept of sexual harassment did not exist for the state or for men. Women recognised the abuse of power by men over women, but this ideology is so deeply rooted in the minds of both that they believed that mixing the genders could create moral degeneration. Thus, they saw the solution as segregation and the state as a location for moral safety.

Fataneh and Maly were both bank workers and identified themselves as middle class with low religious observance. They believed
that

> The state sector has large workplaces where *fesad* can rarely happen. In
> the small, private-sector workplaces, there is a great deal of *fesad*, because
> men and women work closely together. Many women prefer to work
> for the state sector, they feel safer in these large places, both in terms of
> the relationship between the sexes and sexual harassment.

And for Azar, who identified herself as middle class and religious:
'For religious families, women working in the private sector is out
of question. Within the state sector, teaching is the most respectable
profession.' Besides the importance of morality, women also preferred
working for banks and the state sector because the flexibility of
hours allowed women to perform their domestic work more easily.
In the late 1980s and the early 1990s, banks introduced flexible
hours for women who had children. Many women found this help-
ful, as they could work flexible hours for three days a week, even
though they were paid half a full-time salary. These women were
also offered one year's unpaid maternity leave without losing the
security of their job. Although this gap was not included in their
years of service, many women accepted the offer.

Nursing was another profession where women were concentrated.
Working in state hospitals was regarded as preferable although low
wages and bad conditions in the state sector forced poorer women
to work in the private sector or in both. Forough, a 45-year-old
nurse, described her experience:

> I have worked in both private and state hospitals. In some ways nurses
> prefer to work in private hospitals, because conditions of work are less
> harsh than in the state hospitals. The state hospitals are overcrowded,
> there are terrible shortages of medicine, food and equipment. The salaries
> are also higher in the private hospitals. However, there is more job
> security and flexibility in the state hospitals, you have a lifetime job. No
> one can dismiss you providing you keep your head down and do as you
> are told. You don't have this security in the private sector. There is a
> great deal of competition and with the slightest problem you can lose
> your job. But still the harsh conditions of work in the state-run hospitals
> and very low wages force many women to seek jobs in the private
> hospitals.

The choice between the state sector and the private sector was different for women and men. Men chose to work in the state sector because of the material advantages; women for ideological reasons. Even when women considered the material advantages of this sector, the choice was ideologically based. In some cases, economic pressure forces women to work in both sectors or to alternate, but it is the pressure of ideology that controls the supply of their labour.

Gender Segregation within Employment

Interviews revealed some women's responses to sex segregation within employment and the positive and negative effects of this policy. In some cases, segregating women and men in workplaces increased female employment. As discussed in Chapter 3, opportunities opened for a large number of women to be employed in boutiques and shops serving women only. Supervisory positions were created for women in some factories where male and female workers were segregated on assembly-line production. When I visited Bel Air radio and television factory I observed that women worked on one side of the assembly line and men on the other. Zahra, supervisor of the women's assembly line, explained:

> Complete segregation is not always practical. There is a division of labour between female and male workers. Women assemble the smallest items, as they have small fingers, and men carry heavy items. But sometimes to accomplish their task they have to move around and mix with male workers. Since Islamisation we have female supervisors for female workers, like myself, which we did not have before. This is to reduce the amount of contact between the male and female workers but has created higher positions for some women.

Mansoureh, a VDU operator, confirmed:

> There are some positive aspects to segregation. We work in a much more relaxed atmosphere because there is much less sexual harassment. This means that many religious women feel comfortable going out to work, while under the previous system they could not. Before, all supervisors were men; now we have female supervisors, which is good.

Although segregation had created opportunity for some women to become supervisors and managers, their numbers were very small and there was always a man above them. This was to comply with the religious ideology that women should not be judging and managing. The ideological effect of women's priority being the home was to stigmatise women in employment. The ideology of segregation, therefore, imposed social control on women and enforced an inferior position in relation to men. Zohreh, the manager of a laboratory in a chemical industry, explained:

> I am a scientist and I have a great responsibility as the head of the team and the head of the section. I have to control the whole of the production process, from controlling the raw materials, to the control of formulas and packaging. I have eleven specialists who work under my supervision. But because I am a woman, I have to work ten times harder than my male counterpart who has been given a higher position than me. To prove that I am able in my position. I constantly have to translate the latest formulas and research about the most up-to-date ways of producing medicine until they recognise my expertise. The male colleagues get others to do their work for them and with a few speeches and letters prove their ability. After one year, one male colleague has received a company car. After seven years, I have been given access to a car with a driver to drive me from my home to work and return. Their reasoning is that I am a woman and did not need a car, because my husband has a car.

Inferiority in the eyes of the law is the basis for women not being promoted at work. Shahnaz, a university lecturer, said:

> Most heads of departments and principles are male. Teaching is considered the right profession for women but not promotion to a high position in the education system. Women do reach some high positions because of their high standard of education and experience, but there is always a limit for them to go any further. They are not promoted because the criterion for promotion is not education and experience, it is gender ideology. Even if women have a high position they cannot go any further. For example, women never go out of their workplaces to meetings and conferences, meeting other heads of sections and principals. It is not seen as good for women to keep going in and out of their workplace. Whereas male colleagues are constantly after promotion, and they achieve it.

Even when women had the knowledge and expertise, lack of access to information and negotiation placed them in inferior positions, as Zohreh made clear:

Men sit together, talk together and support each other. Women are too busy working hard to prove their abilities. Men make relationships between themselves, from management positions to the security officers at the factory gate. This way they create a support network which allows them to manage all their affairs and step up the ladder of promotion and success. Women are ideologically prohibited from doing this.

Simin, an accountant, also explained how male workers created their own support system and network and excluded women from it, and how segregation had made this easy:

I am the head of industrial accounting. But my managing director never asks me to go with him to discuss the business with the bank manager. He goes with a male accountant. It does not look good if he goes with me. This excludes me from further mobility, while allowing the male accountant who is in a lower position to me to be promoted.

Mahin, a nursery school teacher, and Shahin, a bank clerk, explained how the ideology of segregation controlled women's movement within workplaces. Women's movement was allowed only if it was directly related to their domestic responsibilities. This had a negative affect on their upward mobility within their employment, while men's movement was naturally related to their position and further mobility. They both had similar experiences:

During the break time women never go out, while men go out to meet with other colleagues. If women have to go out, it is usually to deal with their domestic and child-care problems; they have to fill a form and take time off, which is calculated and deducted from their salary. For men, however, it is so normal to go out that it is naturally accepted as going out for business.

Nahid, the technical vice-president of an electronics firm, confirmed that even if women worked better and harder than their male counterparts, segregation limited their mobility within the workforce:

In this factory I am the only female person in the position of management. Male managers usually come late and leave early. But I work 10–12 hours a day to prove my suitability. I never go out to meet any colleagues. I am never invited to meetings and conferences, while I am more knowledgeable about new technology and scientific management than any of my male colleagues.

In the 1980s, female journalists had perhaps the hardest time fulfilling their task under pressure of the ideology of segregation. Going to places, hearing people and engaging in discussions and debates were an important part of a journalist's work; in Iran, female journalists could not do these things because such activities were considered undignified for women. When men did the same it was considered to be part of their knowledge, specialisation and efficiency.[1] Shahrzad, a journalist, explained:

> Many female journalists are forced to accept this attitude. They put their heads down and do what they are told, in order to prove their dignity. A good female journalist is the one who is quiet and her head is down. Those who argue and get involved in discussions and debates are not good women. Female journalists are not sent to other cities or abroad. Unmarried female journalists are in an even worse position. Very few responsibilities are given to them. Married women with children sometimes have to leave early or arrive late because of child-care problems. They usually welcome that they are excluded from being sent to other cities and abroad, otherwise they will be under more pressure for fulfilling their domestic work as well as their journalist tasks. As a result they are given the least important jobs and they are treated badly even if they are good journalists and write well. Women journalists are usually considered unable to do their job properly.

Zhila, another journalist, agreed:

> All editors and heads of section are men. Female journalists' activities are very restricted. They are never sent to other cities, let alone abroad. Ministries and other workplaces mostly stress that they don't want women journalists. I am the only female journalist in the political department. But my male colleagues believe that because I am a female, I am emotional and weak so I cannot do my job effectively. So I have to work much harder to prove that I am a good journalist. They appreciate that I am a good writer. But they send a male colleague to collect information and then they ask me to write and rewrite his material, which will then be published in his name.

Gender segregation had some positive effects. In some cases it increased the supply of female labour and created opportunities for women to rise to positions managing and supervising. But more often segregation imposed social control on women and forced women into an inferior position.

Conclusion

Analysis of my field research data for the second phase of Islamisation (1981–89) suggests that the state used the war to legitimise its hegemony. But the economic circumstances of the war years affected women's expectations, family relations and their positions in the labour market, and consequently had a powerful impact on Islamic ideology concerning female participation in the workforce. The demand for female labour gradually increased in both the state and private sectors of the economy. Women were engaged in a variety of occupations and their contribution was absolutely necessary for the well-being of their families. In this period, the state used different perceptions and the process of segregation as accommodating mechanisms to perpetuate women's employment, despite its stated ideology that women's place is in the home. These mechanisms were then used by the state to control female labour and exclude most women from upward mobility.

Note

1. As will be discussed in Chapter 6, in the 1990s this situation changed and women's participation in the media increased enormously.

Chapter 5

Reversal

The end of the war with Iraq in 1988 and the death of Ayatollah Khomeini in 1989 marked a real reversal of the state's economic gender and employment policies. Despite the initial attempt by the Islamic state to exclude women from employment, a comparison of the statistical data pre-1979 with data from the 1980s and 1990s shows that women's participation in the labour force barely changed. In this period, under socio-economic pressure and women's responses, the state relaxed measures which were initially designed to control women's position in the public sphere. Family law and education and employment regulations were reformed. However, despite these reforms, patriarchal relationships continued to impact on women's employment. Evidence from interviews demonstrates that gendered roles in the domestic domain, women's subjection to men's permission, shortage of nursery schools, gender-blind policies and state intervention to influence the structure of the labour market are among factors ensuring women's subordination within the workforce.

Women in the Economy in the 1990s

A comparison of statistical data for state and privately owned and controlled enterprises in three different periods – before 1979, the mid-1980s and the 1990s – will show the extent to which the Islamic state was able or unable to abolish female labour, as was its stated aim. The figures show that the percentage of female workers in state ministries did not fall – in fact it increased from 29 per cent to 31 per cent. As is shown in Table 5.1, the percentage of women increased

Table 5.1   Female workforce in selected state ministries, selected years (%)

Ministries	1974/5	1986/7	1996/7
Total	29	29	31
Education	41	43	46
Trade	27	8	9
Health	26	41	42
Justice	6	10	27
Higher education	39	19	20
Tourism	27	–	–
Industries	–	5	11
Islamic guidance	–	17	18

Source: Extracted and calculated from Iran Statistical Yearbooks 1977/8: 66; 1986/7: 86; 1996/7: 89.

in the ministries of education, health and justice. It fell in trade and higher education, while the ministry of tourism closed down. However, new ministries were set up under the Islamic administration and the percentage of female workers in the new ministries increased. Also, the number of women employed in the Reconstruction Crusade increased from 579 in 1986/7 to 1,234 in 1989/90; to 1,438 in 1991/2; to 1,751 in 1993/4 and 1,882 in 1995/6 (Iran Statistical Yearbooks 1988/9: 69; 1992/3: 79; 1994/5: 71 and 1996/7: 89).

Statistical information for large industrial enterprises (state and privately owned) employing more than ten workers is available only up to 1993/4. According to these statistics a comparison of 1993/94 with mid-1980s, and pre-revolution figures shows that the number of these enterprises increased from 3,973 in 1972/3 (Iran Statistical Yearbooks 1977/8: 383) to 5,922 in 1993/4 (Iran Statistical Yearbooks 1994/5: 164). In 1993/4 these industries employed 619,437 workers, of whom 34,479 were women and 584,958 were men (Iran Statistical Yearbooks 1994/5: 158), in comparison with 1972/3 when these industries employed 19,459 women and 230,190 men (Iran Statistical Yearbooks 1977/8: 386). Although the number of women workers in these industries increased in the 1980s and early 1990s, women's share of the workforce fell from 8 per cent before 1979 to 6 per cent.

A comparison of pre-1979 figures with 1986/7 figures for small private enterprises shows a fall in the total percentage of women workers in these industries from 9 per cent to 7 per cent, but in 1996/7 it increased to 10 per cent. According to these statistics, women as a proportion of unpaid family workers increased from 17 per cent in 1972/3 to 43 per cent in 1986/7, and to 46 per cent in 1996/7; the share of female wage and salary earners decreased from 10 per cent in 1972/3 to 5 per cent in 1986/7 and then increased to 8 per cent in 1996/7; female self-employed fell from 7 per cent in 1972/3 to 4 per cent in 1986/7 and climbed back to 7 per cent in 1996/7. Women among employers increased from 1 per cent in 1972/3 to 4 per cent in 1986/7 and decreased to 3 per cent in 1996/7, still higher than before 1979 revolution.

However, many of my respondents expressed doubts about the figures for female employment in small private enterprises. First, those who collect statistics, mainly men, do not talk directly to women. Second, as discussed in Chapter 4, many women who may be working as employers, self-employed or unpaid family workers do not declare themselves as workers because they see themselves primarily as housewives. The actual number of women in these enterprises must be higher than the statistics show. Assuming that this problem existed under the Pahlavi, it can be concluded that the percentage of female workers in both state ministries and private enterprises has increased. So this analysis of the sexual division of labour shows that the Islamic state was unable to abolish women's labour. Despite state ideology, women have not been marginalised but are involved in a variety of employment, where their contribution is absolutely necessary to improve the living standards of their families.

Shifts in the Position of the State

The war with Iraq lasted eight years, ending in 1988. Both sides claimed victory. It was estimated that one million Iranians and half a million Iraqis died, and a million others were left physically and psychologically disabled. Ayatollah Khomeini died on 3 June 1989. War reconstruction began and economic relations were liberalised. In the 1990s, the restructuring of the economy was a move towards further integration into the global economy.

Despite the emphasis on Islamic moral, ethical and financial laws, the economic system in Iran rapidly adapted to world capitalism. Islamic economic laws and regulations were modified to allow the operation of a capitalist mode of production based on private owner-ship of the means of production, with an Islamic flavour. For example, production and consumption of alcoholic beverages and pork was prohibited. Nevertheless alcoholic drinks were produced and distributed in the underground economy. While interest was officially prohibited, it was charged in the uncontrolled financial markets of the *bazaar*. Fees, bonuses, prizes and discounts replaced the interest rate in the controlled nationalised banking system (Rahnema and Nomani 1990: 159–61).

However, the absence of an interest rate remained a problem. It did not and still does not operate as a mechanism to adjust inflation. Inflation was, therefore, very high (officially recorded at 40–45 per cent in the 1990s), severely reducing purchasing power. Moreover, the liberalisation of the economy did not lead to economic growth. Productive investment remained low and the currency remained outside world currency markets. The foreign exchange problem created an unstable economy and discouraged entrepreneurs from making long-term investments. Iran's traders exchanged Rials under different exchange rates. Although the state provided a favourable exchange rate for entrepreneurs and traders, these were involved only in short-term investments and trade, making quick profits and moving their profits to foreign banks. The process of impoverish-ment, especially of the poor, who constituted the backbone of the Islamic regime, had been intensified (Behdad 1995a, 1995b; Pessaran 1995; Poya 1991).

Despite these economic problems, the oil money had helped to generate funds. The Gulf War of 1991 and the American destruction of Iraq's economy pushed oil prices up, and Iran benefited. In 1990–92, Iran's oil revenue increased to US$18 billion before falling slightly to US$16 billion. The GDP began to rise, and imports rose from US$11 billion in 1988 to US$24 billion in 1991; as a result, consumption increased (Behdad 1995a; Poya 1991). Thus, the general level of demand for labour increased as a result of post-war reconstruction.

The World Bank's loan of US$250 million in 1991 and a further US$850 million in 1994 indicated further liberalisation of the economy, and were followed by adjustment policies. This meant deregulation to encourage privatisation, removing price controls and cutting subsidies, which gave rise to inflation and unemployment (Behdad 1995a). Under these circumstances, women's earnings became more necessary than ever before to prevent the standard of living of large segments of the population from falling drastically.

In this period the prisoners of war returned. The voluntary work of women in Islamic organisations declined. But in the absence of state welfare to subsidise the unemployed, the war veterans and their families, more opportunities were created for women to participate in the labour force. Priority for training and employment opportunities were given to women who lost men from their families in the war. A large number of women who worked in the Islamic organisations on a voluntary basis were now paid a wage. But state propaganda continued to emphasise part-time work for women. In his speech on Iran's Women's Day, the birthday of Fatimah, in 1991, President Rafsanjani announced the law for part-time work, allowing women to spend half their time in economic activities and the other half performing their domestic duties (Keyhan 26 December 1991). On the same day Ayatollah Khamenei, who replaced Khomeini as spiritual leader, also reminded women that the family was a natural institution and was the basis for women's activities. Women with all their expertise and knowledge must first fulfil their family role (Keyhan 26 December 1991).

The Reform of the Family Law

The end of the war with Iraq in 1988 and Khomeini's death in 1989 coincided with a massive economic and social crisis and with demands for liberalisation of the economy and society. The government-controlled media expressed the changing position of the Islamic state. They reported the statistics about the population explosion and argued that this problem was partly the result of arranged marriages, partly of encouraging marriages 'as a way to combat moral degeneration', and partly of the banning of contraceptives. According to official statistics Iran's population increased from 33,708,744 in 1976/7 to 49,445,010 in 1986/7 and to 60,055,488 in 1996/7 (Iran Statistical Yearbook 1996/7: 33).

In July 1989, the Ministry of Health announced plans for a government policy on population control. In February 1990, Ayatollah Sanei even raised the question of the acceptability of abortion as a method of birth control (*Zane Rouz* 3 February 1990). This was in complete contrast to official policy in the early 1980s, when Ayatollah Khomeini emphasised that 'abortion, regardless of the stage of pregnancy, and sterilisation were prohibited in Islam' (Paidar 1997: 288–9). The media waged a massive campaign for population control. Posters were put up in the streets, factories, offices, schools and universities calling for national awareness of the problem. Newspapers warned about the link between poverty, illiteracy, unemployment and population increase. *Keyhan* newspaper, in a series of articles, reported:

> The total land under cultivation is only 12 million hectares, which is only enough to feed 30 million persons. The rate of population growth among the 6–10 age group is 4.7 per cent per annum. This means that in the last 15 years their number has been doubled. If this trend continues, Iran's school student population will grow to 27 million within the next 20 years. They need employment, which the state cannot provide. One employed person is responsible for feeding 3.5 persons. In order to maintain this level of employment the state has to create 950,000 jobs every year, while between 1976 and 1986 only 190,000 jobs were created. In terms of health, the rate of population increase has been 3 per cent while the rate of increase in opening health centres has been 1.3 per cent. (*Keyhan* 18, 21, 25 September 1991)

The media also criticised the family law for the population explosion:

> The model of having many children means poverty, more people living in shanty towns and higher mortality rates. All the regulations in relation to encouraging the population increase must be abandoned, and health and employment must be improved, as an effective way to decrease population growth. The ministry of health and education must campaign and help people to understand the importance of the use of birth control. Higher budgets should be allocated for females' education, health and employment. (*Keyhan* 22, 23, 26 September 1991)

Table 5.2   Increase in the use of contraception, 1989–91

	Pill	Condom	Coil
1989–90	7,612,350	15,707,136	96,809
1990–91	8,079,933	37,938,343	133,121
% increase	6	141	37

Source: Calculated on the basis of information in *Keyhan* newspaper, 19 September 1991.

The media, especially women's magazines, encouraged the use of contraceptives. Different forms of contraception (the pill, condom, coil and sterilisation) were free of charge and available on demand. *Keyhan* reported that there was widespread backstreet abortion and warned about the dangers of this practice. As is shown in Table 5.2 it also provided information about the percentage increase in the use of different forms of contraception between 1989 and 1991 (*Keyhan* 18–24 September 1991). On 11 March 1992, the same newspaper announced that 330 hospitals around the country were distributing different forms of contraception free of charge. The statistics for annual population growth rate show that the government's population control policy was relatively successful. The annual population growth rate in the mid-1970s was 3 per cent. In the mid-1980s it rose to 4 per cent, but in the mid-1990s it fell again to 1.5 per cent, lower than before the revolution (Iran Statistical Yearbook 1996/97: 33).

Reforms were also made in laws regarding marriage, divorce and custody of children. The High Judicial Council agreed with a new clause in the marriage law, stating that women, at the time of marriage, may request that the clause 'Condition under the Marriage Law' be included in their marriage contract. Under this clause a woman had the right to ask for divorce, refuse the husband the right to marry another woman, and have custody of her children, boys to their adulthood and girls as long as she did not remarry. A man no longer had the unilateral right to divorce his wife simply by registering his will at a registry office without the woman's knowledge; men and women had to go to the civil courts for divorce, and registry offices could register divorce only with a civil court's decree.

Furthermore, war widows, and subsequently other widows, were granted the right to keep and raise their children and were entitled to their husband's wage, salary or living expenses paid by the government, without the interference of male kin. This reform was the result of poorer women challenging the *Sharia* law of guardianship, which gave all custody and legal and financial rights to the male kin after the death of the husband, and demanding its reform.

Also, with the efforts of female lawyers such as Shirin Ebadi and Mehranguiz Kaar and the support of women's journals and newspapers between 1996 and 1999 (see Chapter 6), despite much opposition by the conservative members of the *Majles*, twenty reformed family laws were passed in favour of women. For example, the *mahr* law which is written into the marriage contract, regarding payment to the woman on divorce or after the husband's death, is to be index-linked, with Central Bank of Iran specialists calculating the updated rate of *mahr*. Also, according to the reformed divorce law, if a man decides to divorce his wife unjustly he has to pay compensation *Ojratolmesl* to her – the equivalent of her contribution to the family throughout the years that they lived together. These were particularly important for poorer women, who were either divorced unjustly or after the death of the husband subject to discriminatory and unfair inheritance law.

Similar reform allowed female lawyers to practise family law in the civil courts. The law stated that 'In each civil court a woman who has knowledge of the law must be present to deal with divorce cases' (*Keyhan* 19 October 1991; 25 September 1991; *Zane Rouz* 18 August 1991).

At the 1997 International Conference on Middle Eastern Studies, Mehranguiz Kaar, a female lawyer from Tehran, at a round-table discussion on the situation of women in Iran, argued that,

> After the revolution the religious leaders insisted that in Islamic laws women do not have the right to be judges, and female judges were sacked. In the mid-1990s we have seen a step towards ratifying and returning to the previous situation. There is now a law which allows women to act as judges, but not as judges who give definitive judgement which delineates this part of the law; their signature in this context

is not validated. According to the law women can be research judges. They prepare the case, they prepare the evidence, they prepare the argument and they present it to a male judge who makes the final decision on the basis of the research. This has allowed women lawyers predominantly to act as judges in family law, but by law they can be research judges in different areas. Before this law, according to *Sharia*, women had no right to be judges. Now in practice women are acting as judicial councillors. Remarkably the clergy are now stating that in principle, in Islamic terms, there is no barrier to women acting as full judges and giving full judgement in all cases. For many Iranian women this is a substantial step forward. For this reason we feel that fundamental change is taking place; in this process we have fought very hard to achieve certain reforms, and we are determined not to lose them. We have a permanent foothold, and the way forward is clear.

Furthermore, the Islamic state legitimised male and female relationships outside marriage, through reform of the *sighe* law. President Rafsanjani affirmed that sex outside marriage was not acceptable and, if practised, carried penalties ranging from one hundred lashes to stoning to death, according to the severity of the sin. He argued that *sighe* could resolve the problem of moral degeneration in an Islamic society, but also that *sighe* could resolve the sexual needs of women as well as men. He argued that the practice of temporary marriage had to be made more acceptable; women as well as men could initiate such a marriage. There was no need for the marriage ceremony to be conducted by a clergyman and to be registered in the presence of a witness. The man and the woman could recite the formula, even in Farsi if they found the Arabic version difficult. Through this private verbal contract the man and the woman could be together for any length of time (*Zane Rouz* November 1990).

Throughout November and December 1990 a heated debate took place in the Iranian media about the advantages and disadvantages of this reform. The relatively secular middle classes regarded it as legalised prostitution. Other more religious social groups regarded Rafsanjani's reform as preferable to decadent western-style promiscuity and free love. However, despite the initial attempt by the Islamic state to encourage temporary marriage and President Rafsanjani's reform, the practice remained marginal and stigmatised. Virgin women, in particular, could not initiate *sighe* without jeopardising their future marriageability (Haeri 1989, 1994).

More importantly, changing the law did not easily change people's attitudes. The cultural value attached to the principle of marriage and virginity was so deeply rooted that, despite acknowledging female sexuality and giving less importance to the question of virginity, many were reluctant to accept male–female sexual relationships outside permanent marriage.

The most important effect of this reform, however, was the way some women used it to legitimise their freedom of movement and employment status. Laila explained:

> After getting divorced from my first husband I set up a small media and communication business to publish a literature and art magazine. But it was impossible because I was a divorced woman, living with my two children without a husband. Meanwhile I became fond of a male colleague. We wanted to be together and work together. This was another impossibility. I did not want to marry him. I wanted to get to know him. I, therefore, proposed to him a temporary marriage for a year. Everyone around us disapproved, they thought it was degrading for me. But for me this was the only way to work without being harassed by the neighbours and the people I worked with.

The Reform of the Education System

As noted in Chapter 3, in 1980 all higher education institutions closed down. In 1984, they reopened with the slogan 'Religion before Science', and major changes were introduced. The changes included general criteria for all applicants: believing in Islam or one of the religions recognised by the Islamic Constitution, and having no connection with political parties categorised as anti-government or atheistic. Male applicants also had to meet very strict requirements of military service (Mojab 1987: 6). The aim was to create a totally religious generation (Higgins and Shoar-Ghaffari 1994: 36–40; Matini 1989; *Iran Almanac and Book of Facts Echo of Iran* no. 6 1986).

The criteria for female applicants, however, signified that Islamic gender was ideology in operation. Women were not admitted to a large number of courses. For example, 64 per cent of the institutions did not admit women to mathematical and technical sciences; 17 per cent did not admit women to courses categorised as experimental sciences – these were veterinary sciences, animal science, agrarian studies, geology, disease control and natural resources. Conversely,

Women, Work and Islamism

Table 5.3   Literacy by gender in urban and rural areas, 1976–97

	Urban areas			Rural areas			All areas		
	Total	Female	Male	Total	Female	Male	Total	Female	Male
1976/7	65	56	74	30	17	44	47	35	59
1986/7	73	65	80	48	36	60	62	52	71
1996/7							79	74	85

Source: Extracted and calculated from Iran Statistical Yearbooks 1992: 113, 1996/7: 515.

midwifery, family hygiene and sewing as part of art and design courses admitted only women. In other areas the maximum limits for female applicants ranged between 25 per cent to 50 per cent (Mojab 1987: 7). Finally, in 1985, the Majles passed a law which prohibited unmarried women from going abroad to study. Their underlying philosophy was that they may be affected by western values and cultures.

However, in the second half of the 1980s and in the 1990s the education system was reformed, allowing women greater participation in previously restricted fields of study. As is shown in Table 5.3, although the female literacy rate lagged behind the male, the gap was narrowing, especially in urban areas, in comparison with the pre-1979 period. A detailed analysis of women's education in the Islamic Republic shows that it increased at all levels in both urban and rural areas, with the exception of middle school, as shown in Table 5.4. This was despite all the limitations of Islamic gender ideology and the state's intention to seclude women in the home.

The percentage increase in female education was not homogeneous for all urban and rural areas. When I visited a number of villages in the east and the north of Iran in 1991, I learned that in the poor areas of the east very few girls went to school, but in the comparatively richer areas of the north most girls went to school alongside boys. This was a change from the first phase of Islamisation, when educational segregation excluded female children from going to school in rural areas. Nevertheless, as is also shown by Higgins and Shoar-Ghaffari's detailed analysis of women's education in poorer

Table 5.4   Female education in selected years (% girls)

Education level	Urban areas			Rural areas			All areas		
	1976/7	1986/7	1996/7	1976/7	1986/7	1996/7	1976/7	1986/7	1996/7
Primary school	40	45	45	27	39	48	35	43	46
Middle school	50	43	41	26	30	35	43	38	39
Secondary school	37	43	46	19	24	30	35	40	44
Higher education	27	29	34	15	14	19	26	28	33
Total	38	43	45	26	36	45	35	40	45

Source: Extracted and calculated from Iran Statistical Yearbooks 1981/2: 113; 1989/90: 108; and 1996/7: 516.

parts of the country and in non-Persian ethnic provinces, the educational level was generally low, and female education especially so. But here, too, the gap was narrowing (Higgins and Shoar-Ghaffari 1994).

To analyse gender differentiation by area of specialisation I have compared men's and women's degrees in different fields of study (medicine, humanities, science, technical and engineering, agriculture, arts and architecture) for the academic years 1992/3–1993/ 4 and 1996/7–1997/8. As shown in Table 5.5, more women than men studied medicine at some levels of further and higher education. In other areas the reverse was the case because priority was given to male students, and these fields were considered unsuitable for women. Nevertheless the gap was narrowing.

The establishment of Alzahra University, for women only, played an important role. The lecturers had exploited the idea of the university as a single-sex institution and had opened up opportunities for women to study many courses not available in other universities. Fatemeh, head of a department, explained:

Alzahra university, the only female university in Iran, provides many science degree courses for females and has increased the number of female students in many higher degree courses. However, in other universities there are many courses which are closed to women. For example chemistry, physics, medicine, dentistry and biology courses

Table 5.5   Women taking further and higher education degrees in different fields of study (%)

	Higher diploma	BA/BSc	MA/MSc	PhD
1992/3–1993/4				
Medicine	51	71	55	40
Humanities	12	32	15	13
Science	20	38	19	22
Technical and engineering	3	7	4	4
Agriculture	1	3	3	8
Arts and architecture	47	45	20	7
1996/7–1997/8				
Medicine	67	66	49	45
Humanities	41	40	19	17
Science	27	45	24	18
Technical and engineering	7	14	5	5
Agriculture	21	29	3	7
Arts and architecture	74	49	22	29

Source: Extracted and calculated from Iran Statistical Yearbooks 1995: 471–2 and 1996/7: 558.

give priority to male students. This is even written in the handbooks for entry examination to university degree courses, which in reality closes many doors to women's education and employment.

The regulations forbidding females to study agricultural studies (*Keyhan* 16 May 1989) and law (*Keyhan* 25 September 1991) were also modified, creating more opportunities for women in these fields. According to the Ministry of Higher Education, 52 per cent of those students who passed the September 1998 universities' entry examination (*Konkour*) and entered university in the academic year 1998/9 were women.

These reforms were a result of pressure on the state applied by women who had to participate in the labour market despite Islamic ideology. For example, in 1990 religious women objected to the 1985 education law which prevented unmarried female students from studying abroad. They argued that they supported the Islamic state, but that their interests were defined in both gender and class terms, and that the Islamic state was failing them by ignoring their interests. A group of these women wrote a letter to *Keyhan*:

> This law discriminates against religious working-class women who rely for their studies on government financial help. Those women who have money can go abroad despite the law and continue their education. It is also gender discrimination, because why should moral degeneration only apply to women and not to men? We appreciate the importance of marriage and for this reason we appeal to the *Majles* to reform the law and allow women over 28 who have a good record of Islamic behaviour to be allowed to continue their higher education abroad. (*Keyhan* 22 November 1990)

In the 1980s, the state policy of sex segregation in sports was successful, and women's sport suffered severely. However, in the 1990s, women-only sports grounds were created for swimming, table-tennis, horse riding, skiing, shooting and chess. The state also allowed women to compete internationally in sports, such as flat-water kayaking, that did not require compromising the *hejab* (*Guardian* 1 November 1995).

The interaction between ideological factors and material circumstances has changed gender consciousness and attitudes to female education. Many families regard higher education as a valuable asset for women as well as for men. The ideal future is seen to depend on being a university graduate. The idea of 'marriage after university; work after university; independence after university' is becoming a shared value expressed by many young women. Although many female graduates do not enter the workforce, as their priority is to get married and have children, many young women's attitude is 'if I do not get married, I will get a job' (Farhadpour 1998). This is also evident in the statistics for the age of marriage. Although officially the age of consent for girls is 9, in practice the average age of marriage is 22 in both urban and rural areas (Iran Statistical Yearbook 1996/7: 62).

> The *Sharia* law is contradictory with civil law. For example, according to *Sharia* law 9-year-old girls can get married. According to education law,

all children aged 7 must go to school, otherwise their parents can be punished for not respecting the civil law of compulsory education for children. Also conventionally a 9-year-old is considered a child. This is one of the contradictions which have united all women, regardless of their class and levels of religious observance, to pressurise the state for reform. (Kaar 1997)

Patriarchal Relationships and Women's Employment

The initial changes made to underwrite patriarchal relations in the public and private spheres of life did not seclude women within the home and, as discussed previously, the state had to change its position and reform the laws and regulations. However, as I argued in Chapter 1, Kandiyoti's characteristics of classic patriarchy (1991: 31–5) are more prevalent in Iran under the Islamic state than under the Pahlavi. The ideology of the patrilocal household and the authority of the senior man has been strengthened. Even in prosperous urban areas, such as Tehran, economic hardship had forced many young families to abandon their nuclear unit and live with their parents. Azar, a school teacher, explained:

> We live with my husband's family firstly because we cannot afford to have a place of our own; secondly, because my husband works outside Tehran most of the time and in the eyes of my husband's family it is not good that I live on my own. They are a religious family. They don't like the idea that I work outside the home but there is not much choice, as we need the money. To compensate for this I have to do most of the housework. My brother-in-law and his family also live in the same household. My sister-in-law and I share the housework between us. She sometimes helps me with my son. For example, if I cannot take him to school or collect him on time, she does it for me. As a result, I end up doing most of the housework for three families.

The cultural value attached to marriage and total compliance with the practice of *mahr* and *nafaghe* had increased to the extent that their practice is a source of prestige and to deviate from them is to dishonour the family. Minoo explained:

> I was a student in London and there I lived with my boyfriend. When we returned to Tehran, under pressure from our families we had to get married. Before the marriage ceremony our families bargained over the rate of my *mahr* for a long time and finally agreed a price. I had to go

along with this degrading practice because in the eyes of my family I have already dishonoured myself and my family by losing my virginity to a man and living with him without being married to him. My mother wanted to regain my honour and the honour of our family. She was satisfied by succeeding in getting my husband's family to agree to the amount of my *mahr* being equal to my husband's sister (my sister-in-law), who was married a few months ago.

In rural areas, in particular, many poorer women were forced to marry older men in order to survive poverty and deprivation. Zahra, a young carpet-weaver and agricultural worker, explained:

My family, who live in the next village, are very poor; they have no land of their own and work as agricultural workers. Three years ago they married me to my husband who is 70 years of age, because they couldn't afford to keep me any more. My husband owns his land. I gave him a son. He has six older children from his first marriage. His daughter, Maryam, is older than me. But he likes to have more children.

Marriage of cousins had also become more common than during the 1960s and 1970s. Segregation of the sexes in public places led to a situation where public gathering and entertainment were non-existent. There is divided seating in most public places such as cinemas, theatres and concert halls. Only those who were married to each other or related through the extended family could sit together in the restaurants or walk together in the streets, parks, mountains and other public places. People's movements were strictly under the surveillance of the Islamic security forces. The degree of punishment for non-conformity varied between imprisonment, eighty lashes and severe warning. As a result, the extended family gathering was almost the only form of entertainment. This situation had reduced the chances of men and women meeting and getting to know each other.

If women were not married and had no children, they were expected to look after the old and the sick within their family. Shahin is a 40-year-old administrative officer:

After my divorce, everyone in my family expected me to look after my old and sick parents instead of continuing my education and seeking a career through employment, especially as I had no children. As a result I have been looking after my parents for many years. Since my mother died I have been looking after my father and for the last two years I

have been working part-time, in the afternoons, in my brother's company. I wake up at 7 a.m., make breakfast for my father, give him his
medicines, do cleaning, washing, shopping and cooking. After lunch I
give my father his medicines and put him to bed for an afternoon nap
and then I go out to work. At work I have a large number of responsibilities, administrative work, secretarial work and telephone operator.
I also help with the VDU operators, planners, accountant and the librar-
ian. Everybody expects me to work harder because I am not married
and have no children. They seem to forget that looking after a sick old
man is as demanding as looking after a child. I end up working at the
weekends and on public holidays. I work harder than my brother, who
is the managing director of the company. I feel that if I was not a
woman and I was not expected to look after my parents, I should have
been the managing director.

A married woman had prestige and social status; a single or
divorced woman had neither. Women's virginity was the most important factor determining the honour of the husband and the family.
Mally explained how these values forced women to abandon their
children for the honour of the family:

> When I was sixteen I married and I have a son from that marriage. After
> a few years my husband divorced me to marry another woman. Life
> was hell, because I was a divorced woman and had a child on my own.
> I met my second husband. He was also divorced and had a son from his
> first marriage. It appeared that it could be an equal relationship, but it
> was not and is not. When we decided to marry, he told me that his
> family's honour would be in jeopardy if they found out that I was not
> a virgin, a divorced woman with a child. I had no choice but to hide
> this reality and send my son to be brought up by my mother. Since then
> I have been pretending that he is my younger brother. But my husband
> does not have this problem; he regularly meets his son, who lives with
> his mother, and he does not need to lie about him.

The state reformed some laws, but patriarchal control over women
was essential because of the link between the honour of the family
and the honour of the community and society, for which women
were responsible. Thus, if women had to participate in the workforce, and if this threatened the patriarchal authority of the man or
men within the family, the state was going to ensure the operation
of patriarchy at the level of the state and the family. The slogans on
the walls and outside workplaces read: 'Sister, your *hejab* is more
effective than my blood', signed 'on behalf of martyred soldiers of

Islam' (soldiers who died in the war with Iraq); 'Women who are not observing the proper *hejab* are offering their sexuality'; 'Women who do not observe the proper *hejab*, show how dishonourable their men are' (*Maiyar* 1995, no. 14). Also, as discussed earlier, women responded to economic forces, and the reversal of the state's position provided better opportunities for women to enter employment. However, their position as major or auxiliary contributors to the family income was not recognised.

Gendered Roles in the Domestic Domain

As discussed in Chapter 3, the authorities used the concepts of *mahr* and *nafaghe* to justify women's place in the home, performing domestic duties. Under economic pressure women went out to work, but the ideology of female domesticity put them in a disadvantaged position within the labour market. Maryam, a teacher and the mother of four children, explained:

> It was so hard to work as a PE teacher and at the same time be solely responsible for the housework and looking after the children, as my husband never took any responsibility. In the morning I had to rush, take children to my mother and go to work. When I finished work, I had to do shopping, collect children and go home, cook, clean, wash and help with my children's homework. I was always exhausted. As a PE teacher I was expected to be fit and lively, but I wasn't. Most female PE teachers are in the same situation. Some headmistresses were sympathetic, most headmasters were not. As a result most of the time I was demoted. This meant that I had to work in rough working-class areas with fewer resources, while male PE teachers were promoted to middle-class areas with more resources.

Moreover, the ideological effect of the institution of marriage and the concepts of *mahr* and *nafaghe* gave the responsibility for domestic work exclusively to women. The Islamisation of the state and the emphasis on women's place in the home had meant that the only domestic work that men were willing to help with was shopping, which was an activity outside the home, and carrying heavy objects, which was seen as masculine. Mahin is a 33-year-old nursery-school teacher: 'I do all the house work. The only work that my husband is willing to do is shopping and carrying the paraffin and the gas containers from one floor to another.'

This was also because of gender-based processes of socialisation. The majority of men lived before marriage with their family, where their mothers or other women did the domestic work. Fataneh, a 37-year-old nursery-school teacher, said:

> My husband, my children and I live with my parents, who own the house. My sister is also living with us. My mother does all the housework. My sister and I help her when we return home from work. My husband and my father don't touch anything; if they attempt to do anything, it is bound to go wrong. Housework is not men's work. They don't know how to do it and women should respect this. I teach my daughter how to do the housework but not my son.

Attitudes to domestic work differed according to women's access to resources and religious commitment. The poorer the women were, and the more devout, the harder they worked and the longer their hours. In rural areas work was totally household-centred and there was little distinction between their productive work, which was sold in the market by men, and their domestic work. When I asked Ameh Khanom, a 57-year-old agricultural worker and carpet-weaver, if men do any domestic work, she lowered her voice and whispered in my ears that: 'It is wrong if men do any housework. Housework is naturally woman's work. It is a disgrace if men do the housework. Only if something goes wrong with the electricity or the water pump, then it is men's job to fix them.' In a group interview at Margarin factory all seven women that I interviewed explained that they and their daughters or daughters-in-law carried out the domestic work, but not sons, sons-in-law or husbands. They also thought that it would be a disgrace if men did the housework, even though they were unemployed and stayed at home all day while their wives or daughters worked in the factory. The idea of men sitting at home and women going out to work was such a disgrace for these women that they voluntarily approached the management to make them unemployed and give their jobs to their husbands and sons.

Women with better access to resources spend less time on domestic work, but ideologically they were responsible for it. Nahid, the technical vice-president of an electronics firm, aged 33, explained, 'I have a servant who does all the housework. But if she is not around for any reason I do all the housework myself. Mainly because my husband does not know how to do it.' Domestic work was crucial to the standard of living of all families. Men and children depended on women to do this work for them and benefited from it. This division of labour, however, increased women's hours, regardless of their access to resources. Many women did four hours' housework on top of twelve hours' labour a day. Only a minority of urban women, who had chosen to be unmarried and had no children and had made a hard decision to concentrate on their upward mobility through a career, could escape domestic work.

Men's Permission

Despite reforms, it is a convention according to *Sharia* that women must obtain permission from their husbands and/or another male head of the family to seek employment or to be employed. All the women that I interviewed had to obtain such permission to go out to work. The majority of my respondents explicitly stated that they would stop working the moment their husbands asked them to. This is to comply not only with the state regulation but also with the ideology. In the majority of cases men do give permission, mainly because women's earnings are essential for the family's survival.

Class and religious observance play an important role in the practice of such a stance. For example, those women who identify themselves as *Kargar* with high religious devotion are poorer women whose families need their earnings. Under these circumstances, and despite the ideology, men and women have to accept that women must go out to work. As a result male permission is pure formality. When I interviewed a number of women factory workers and agricultural workers/carpet-weavers and asked them about how they obtained permission from their male kin, they looked at me as if I was asking a strange question, and then laughed and said 'men have to give permission, there is no choice'.

Of those who identified themselves as middle class, those with a greater degree of religious observance suffered subordination the most. They practised the values attached to Islamic gender ideology to a greater extent. If a woman had to go out to work, they felt under enormous pressure. Maryam, a nurse, explained:

> I will not work unless I have my husband's permission. My husband and I believe that my prime duty is my domestic activity. We therefore

both feel uneasy about my work as a nurse. To be *khanomeh khaneh* (the lady of the home) and *aghayeh biroon* (the master of outside the home) is a difficult task. It is like trying to run two hostile worlds and keep them in harmony. But we have no choice. My salary is important for the survival of the family.

Another Maryam, a teacher, expressed similar feelings:

We are a religious family. In religious families, women should not go out to work. But we had no choice, I had to go out to work in order to help to feed the family. I had a good opportunity to get a job in a bank. But my brother would not give me permission. He said that it was a disgrace for him if I work, especially in the same workplace. I became a teacher. When I married it was the same story; my husband did not want me to go out to work, but because of financial problems he had to agree that I continue with my job as a physical education teacher. However, he would not agree that I go to games on Fridays (the weekend in Iran). He wouldn't agree that I teach at boys' schools. As a result, I lost overtime pay, bonuses and any opportunity to be promoted. Most female teachers faced the same problems, while male teachers had none of these problems on their path of upward mobility.

Women who identified themselves as 'non-religious middle class', however, were under less ideological pressure from men and the family, and because they had better access to material resources the question of a husband's permission was implicit rather than explicit. They had to comply with the law and to acknowledge male domination within the marriage and the family, but they had a greater degree of autonomy in making decisions about their labour. Maly, the head of a section in a bank, said, 'For the non-religious middle class, it is prestigious that women go out to work and their work is valued, but they are expected to give priority to domestic duties. Women who work are respected, they have more control over their property, belongings and decision making.'

Shortage of Nursery Schools

In 1990 there were only 930 nurseries across the country under the supervision of the ministry of health, 300 of which were privately owned and controlled, and in Tehran, the capital city (*Keyhan* 6 January 1992). Less than half a million children (out of a potential fifteen million) attended such nurseries (*Keyhan* 27 July 1991).

There were three different forms of nursery school in Iran: workplace, state and private. Some large industrial enterprises (employing more than ten workers) had workplace nursery schools. They accepted children under 7 (school age) and were free of charge. Each woman worker had the right to take three of her children to these nursery schools. For others, she was paid up to 8,000 Rials for each child to be looked after in state nurseries outside the factory. Some workplaces, such as banks, schools, hospitals and some ministries, also had nursery schools. They were not free but they were subsidised. The majority of state-sector workplaces that I visited had such nurseries, but many women could not afford to pay even the subsidised fees. Fataneh, mother of two and a bank clerk, explained: 'The workplace nursery charges between 4,000 and 12,000 Rials per month, per child. It was too expensive for me. Most of the time my mother and mother-in-law looked after my children. Otherwise it would have been impossible for me to go out to work.' There were also nurseries subsidised by the state. They charged more than the workplace nurseries within the state sector. But they were overcrowded, with forty-five children in each age group, which was against the labour law. According to the ministry of health, each age group must not exceed thirty children (Keyhan 9 January 1992). They did not have qualified staff and there was evidence of health and educational hazards in many of these institutions (Keyhan 14 January 1992). Article 78 of the employment law, ratified in October 1991, states that all workplaces that employ women must have a nursery school operating under the supervision of the ministry of health. The employer must allow women workers to breast-feed their babies every three hours, for half an hour. Furthermore, these hours should not be deducted from their wages or salaries (Keyhan 7 January 1992). Despite this law, the shortage of child-care provision by the state is an obstacle to women working.

In a series of articles in 1992, Keyhan reported a number of complaints made by women. Nursery fees had increased by 30–50 per cent. This meant that a large number of women could not go out to work. As a result, families' standard of living had fallen. If the government was keen to return women to employment and use their expertise, it must provide nursery facilities (Keyhan 8 January 1992). Women demanded that the government either had to provide

Table 5.6 Women's options for child-care facilities

Type of facilities	Questionnaire	Interviews
Female kin	237	43
Workplace nursery	20	10
State nursery	27	12
Private nursery	8	5

Source: Calculated on the basis of 348 questionnaires and 76 interviews.

better, cheaper state nursery schools or increase their wages so that they could afford private nurseries fees (*Keyhan* 5–14 January 1992).

Private nursery fees varied. The cheapest was 30,000 Rials per month per child, an equivalent of one month's salary for a low-paid worker in the early 1990s. In 1992, a year after the ratification of the labour law stating that workplaces employing women must provide nursery schools, many of these nurseries had to close down from under-use and lack of profit. Many state and workplace nurseries also closed down because of general economic recession (*Keyhan* 27 July 1991). High taxation, high insurance premiums, low pay for workers, high rates, high rent, shortage of appropriate food, lack of technology for disabled children and of general nursery-school resources were identified as reasons for closure (*Keyhan* 7 January 1992). The response of some employers to women's objections to lack of nurseries was, 'we have more important things to do'. Some increased women's wages, but women complained that this did not cover the cost of nurseries. For example, some employers agreed to pay 3,000 Rials per month per child, one-tenth of nursery fees (*Keyhan* 7 January 1992).

Most women whom I interviewed and most of my questionnaires showed that women used their mothers or mothers-in-law to look after their children. For most women any form of nursery school which charged a fee was too expensive. Maryam, a teacher with four children, said, 'Without my mother it would have been impossible for me to go out to work. I could neither afford the expensive private nursery schools nor accept the overcrowded and poor condition of state nurseries.' The shortage of nursery schools reduced the supply of female labour. Paid maternity leave was three months for the first and the second child and one month for subsequent children. But most women took one or two years' unpaid maternity leave, until the children were old enough to be left with their female kin. This put women at a disadvantage in the labour market and had a negative effect on their grade, salary, years of service, insurance, and pension. Mansoureh, a 35-year-old VDU operator, explained:

> I have two children. I have lost two years of service, as I had to take two years' unpaid leave, one for each child. Most women in our workplace are in the same position. We lose years of service for bringing up children. I have worked the same number of years as some of my male colleagues, but, because I have lost two years bringing up children, I am behind of them in terms of grade and salary.

Fataneh, a 48-year-old bank clerk had a similar experience: 'I have four children, I had to take seven years' unpaid leave to bring them up at different times. As a result I have lost seven years of service, affecting my insurance, pension and all other benefits and bonuses.'

Gender-blind Policies

The state's laws and regulations were both gender-based and gender-blind. They placed constraints on women's labour but did not take into consideration women's domestic responsibilities, simply adding to their hours of work. For example, Lily, a 29-year-old secretary, explained how segregation on the buses – one-third of the bus was for women only – added to women's hours of work:

> Going to work with two children was very difficult. I had to take one child to his school and the other to his nursery school. Since they segregated the buses, only one-third of the seats on each bus is allocated to women, on the basis that fewer women go out to work than men. Even if this is the case, they do not consider that this is not enough for women with two, three, four or five children going to work early in the morning. My children and I had to leave the house two hours earlier every morning. By the time I got to work I felt exhausted.

A black market and a ration system introduced during the Iran–Iraq war continued into the 1990s. The black (or free) market reflected the scarcity of imported or import-based products demanded by those who could afford to receive these products at official prices. The ration system reflected the scarcity of goods, mainly food products, which were subsidised by the state. The majority of the population relied on the ration system; without it their standard of living would have been diminished severely. However, as Tahereh, a 28-year-old secretary, explained, the rationing system added to women's hours of work:

> To do the shopping within the rationing system is a great task. One coupon has to be taken to the north of Tehran and another to the south in order to buy the necessities cheaper than on the black market. If you don't go on time your coupons will be out of date. Sometimes it becomes impossible to do the work outside the home as well as the housework and help children with their studies.

In October 1990 the hours of work of state-sector employees changed from 7 a.m.–3 p.m. to 9 a.m.–5 p.m. In a number of articles in newspapers and magazines women described the enormous problems this created:

> I have two children, 5 and 7 years of age. With the change in the hours of work I do not see my children from 7 a.m. to 7 p.m. I am not able to help them with their homework.

> Nursery schools only keep children up to 3–4 p.m. We have no choice other than to bring our children to work until 5 p.m. This is creating problems for us in the workplace.

> Before the change in the hours of work I finished work at the same time as the nursery school. This allowed me to collect my children on the way home. Now I have to take leave to collect my children, which is deducted from my wages. (*Keyhan* 22 October 1990; *Zane Rouz* 12 October 1990)

Shahin, one of my respondents, expressed similar worries:

> Before the change in hours of work I had more time to do the housework. Now I get home around 5.30. I do the cleaning, the washing and the cooking. After dinner I help children with their homework and get them ready for bed. I then have to cook tomorrow's lunch for my children because they only go to school half a day, and also do the

ironing and other bits and pieces. I sometimes find myself working until 1 or 2 in the morning. I don't get enough sleep and I am always very tired.

The Structure of the Labour Market

One important effect of gender ideology was the refusal to recognise women as breadwinners. Therefore their benefits were calculated as for a single person. A single person received half of a married person's allowances and subsidies. For example, employers paid 3,000 Rials per month to a single person and 7,000 Rials to a married person in the form of goods or food subsidies. Sometimes, instead of a cash bonus, coupons were given for food items. These coupons could be sold on the black market if they were not needed for household use, adding a considerable amount to the family income.

Women with children did not receive child benefit. Married women did not receive the married person's allowance. This reduced their salary drastically in comparison with men's. For the same reason, women's tax, pension and retirement deductions and allowances were also calculated as for a single person. For example, after her death a woman's pension would stop, while a man's pension would be transferred to his family. Women and men were entitled to health schemes, but women could use the scheme only for themselves and not for their families. Fataneh explained:

> Banks have their own annual bonus schemes, which is not a part of the national agreement. It is an arbitrary amount which is paid to the employees. Many women do not receive this bonus because they are not considered to be the head of their family. Under special circumstances some women may receive some bonus, but much less than men.

In 1990 *Zane Rouz* published an article describing the government's approval of the new-year bonus to workers. This also revealed the gender differential treatment within the labour force and the labour market. 'Each employee who is married and has children will receive 100,000 Rials. Each employee who is not married will receive 70,000 Rials. Married women are considered as single persons' (*Zane Rouz* 4 March 1990).

According to my field research, exclusion from the category of breadwinner and from benefits and subsidies left women's earnings at half to three-quarters that of their husbands. Moreover, women spend all of their earnings on the household. Men earn more and spend less of their earnings on household expenditure and, therefore, save more. Fatemeh explained:

> I earn 70,000 Rials per month. I pay the rent, which is 30,000 Rials per month and, after consulting my husband, I spend the rest on household expenditure. My husband earns 100,000 Rials per months. I think I pay half of the household expenditure and he pays the other half. He must make some savings.

In some cases where women had access to resources and were less constrained by ideology, they were able to spend less and save more. Fereshteh explained:

> As an electrical engineer and supervisor, I earn 200,000 Rials per month. My husband, who has the same level of education, is a manager and earns 300,000 Rials per month, because he is the breadwinner. I spend very little of my money on household expenditure; I spend it on what I want and I mostly save. I do, however, consult my husband about what I would be spending my money on, because tradition and the norm dictates to me that I should respect him and get his approval.

Zanan monthly magazine reported another way in which women were disadvantaged. Within the state sector 18 per cent of women had higher education, compared with only 6 per cent of men. But only 3 per cent of these women occupied high positions. The article reported the opinions of a number of women in high positions. Dr Firouzeh Khalatbari, assistant director of economic affairs of the Bank Markazi Iran (the central bank), said: 'This is not surprising. In a patriarchal developing country it is natural that the criterion for reaching high status is not superiority in educational level.' Dr Jaleh Shadi, a sociologist at Tehran University, expressed a similar view: 'encouraging women to retire early, the media portraying women as mothers and wives, not allowing women to work in managerial positions, and not considering women as the breadwinners of their families are a few reasons among many to explain why there are few women occupying high positions.' The article also confirmed that many married women had to pay higher tax because they were not considered breadwinners. Nahid Javanmard, barrister and lecturer in employment law, business law and civil law at Azad University, pointed out that, 'In the eyes of the law, men and women may be equal but the employers treat women and men differently' (*Zanan* 22 November 1990).

In the late 1980s and 1990s the state attempted economic expansion and had to respond to pressures of war, economic dislocation and rigidities in the labour market. Expediency replaced the initial hard ideological line with a pragmatic acceptance of an increase in the female labour force. Nevertheless the social relations of gender remained tightly controlled by men and by the state.

Chapter 6

Women's Responses to Patriarchy

The legal reform which had taken place was the result of women's activities inside and outside the country, of activists and scholars who had constantly struggled for change. These struggles had ensured that it was no longer possible to offer the kind of traditional interpretation of Islamic laws that was entirely detrimental to women. (Kaar 1997)

During the years 1979–81, religious and secular women saw the revolution as a first step towards liberation from the uneven economic and political developments of the Pahlavi state. This was mainly an urban movement, especially in big industrial cities such as Tehran. The majority of women in this movement were waged workers, including industrial workers who were engaged in workers' struggles within the workers' councils (*shoras*). After the establishment of the Islamic state, secular women's organisations were driven underground or disappeared, and *shoras* were replaced by Islamic Societies. Throughout the 1980s only religious women's organisations and actions were favoured by the state, and only in the interest of the war efforts. However, by the late 1980s many religious women were politicised. Their experience in paid and unpaid work and their active participation in political movements raised their consciousness about the limitations of Islamic gender relations. In the 1990s, many religious women who supported the Islamic state and opposed the secular women's movement in the first phase of Islamisation changed their position and invited secular women to join them in the debate on women's issues within the media and politics. For many secular women, the Islamic state severely limits their struggle for a better

society free from religion. They see the state holding on to patriarchal gender relations, as its survival depends on them. However,
under this theocratic state, where they have no access to the political
sphere, some secular women see their unity with religious women
as the only way to challenge the Iranian state. In previous chapters
I argued that women actively participated in and responded to economic processes and forced the state to adapt its ideological position and practices. Here I focus on the forms those responses and
struggles have taken. A combination of women's political activism
and individual survival strategies led to gender consciousness on a
scale never before experienced in Iran. Through an analysis of class
and religious consciousness, my aim is to show how women's organised and individual responses constitute a form of constraint on
state power and the patriarchal power of men.

Mass Participation of Women in the Revolution of 1979

Why did women of different social classes and with different levels
of religious observance participate on a mass scale in the 1979 revolution? During this period, millions of women took part in daily
demonstrations, most wearing the black chador. The majority were
religious women who, as noted in Chapter 2, were considered
backward and had no place under the Pahlavi regime. Many young
women of these families had been forced to imitate western values,
including wearing the latest European fashions, when they went to
work or to university, whilst their families insisted that they should
behave according to religious values, including wearing the chador.
This imbalance resulted in a crisis for them. Their support for
Ayatollah Khomeini was a political act against alienation and dissatisfaction, reflecting their anger. More importantly, as I learned
when I interviewed a number of these women, behind the passive
image given to them by the media and the state – they were serving
God and men – was another reality, of strong women taking initia-
tives, organising and raising the consciousness of men and women
about injustice and inequality.

One of my respondents was Azam Taleghani, a member of the
Majles during the revolutionary period of 1979–81, and head of the

Women's Society of the Islamic Revolution. She described women's activities during the revolution:

> Women carried their children on their shoulders and attended meetings, conferences and marches. Many were killed during the street demonstrations against the Shah's regime. We worked in hospitals day and night and looked after the injured. Women left their homes and their husbands to work in hospitals and in the mosques. They only went home a few hours a day to sort out things for their children. Those who had young children organised collective child-care facilities in the neighbourhood, allowing time for everyone to do their share of voluntary work. Women attacked police stations and barracks, confiscated arms and distributed them amongst the revolutionaries.

Forough, another participant in the revolutionary movement, explained how, in her neighbourhood, women took the initiative to work in the hospitals. They forced men to accept their work outside the home, and made them contribute financially to the cause:

> My uncles are *bazaar* merchants. I phoned them one day and told them that I and many other women, rich and poor, from the neighbourhood have decided to go and help the injured in the hospitals. I told them that they should make themselves useful and send us a large amount of cotton materials. They listened and we women sat by our sewing machines, and within a day or two we had cut the materials they sent and made a massive amount of bandages. We washed them, ironed them and took them to hospitals.

It should be noted that the mass movement also included secular women. Even the women members of the Women's Organisation of Iran (the Pahlavi state-sponsored women's organisation) supported the movement, despite the fact that their headquarters were burnt down by the Islamists (Sanasarian 1982: 117). Many women joined the demonstrations every day without the *chador*, and every day were given scarves by the march organisers, who pleaded with them to wear them as a sign of unity for the overthrow of the Shah. One woman activist showed me a whole wardrobe full of scarves which she collected on the demonstrations. This gave the women's response to the revolution an Islamic flavour.

What was important for all these women, religious or secular, was the fact that they all felt that this was the time to fight for change. Parvaneh summed it all up:

Many friends were in jail and under torture. Many were executed. I was anti-Shah, but there was no concrete political guidance for my generation. I found religion as a way of survival. I was not fundamentally religious. I prayed, but I wore a miniskirt. I fasted, but broke my fast with a sandwich and a Coca-Cola in the cinema. I found religion fulfilling and securing my life, but I did not like the religious implication that women should stay at home. I did not want to stay at home. I wanted to be educated and be an artist. (Poya 1992: 149)

Most women, despite differences of class and religious belief, celebrated the revolution and took it to be a first step towards improving their status within the family, employment and the wider society.

Women's Struggle in the Shoras

The 1979 revolution provided an opportunity for trade union activities. An important feature of the early days was the rise of the *shoras*. Women's participation in them raised gender consciousness, as their struggle for better wages and conditions had a gender dimension. The *shoras* survived for eighteen months and played an important political role in securing basic trade union rights in Iran. In rural areas, where the impact of the revolution was not as great as in the urban areas, confrontation between landlords and agricultural workers became widespread, and *shoras* were set up to redistribute land to agricultural workers and to organise production. In oil and other established industries where trade unions existed, some workers' memories of their own or their parents' or close relatives' involvemens in the working-class activism of the 1940s and 1950s helped in the formation of these *shoras*. In industries where the workforce had largely migrated from the rural areas since the 1960s, *shoras* could not be created on the basis of historical experience; the pre-revolutionary strike committees formed the basis of these *shoras* (Bayat 1987: 109–13).

A few days after the revolution, Khomeini sent a message to the workers asking them to go back to work in the name of Islam and revolution. The workers went back, but they found no change – the same wages, and the same conditions. They reacted quickly. In many factories, the manager or the owner had fled the country; their absence provided an opportunity for the workers immediately to create *shoras*. In those factories that had the same management, the same supervisor and even the same SAVAK representatives, this became the reason for the creation of the *shoras*. The workers formed committees within *shoras* to secure different demands, including better wages and conditions, health and insurance, participation in decision making, contact with other *shoras*, publicity for workers' news, the organisation of strike funds and the establishment of women's committees dealing with women's specific demands (Bayat 1987: 102–12; Poya 1987: 143–9).

Soon the independent role of the *shoras* was undermined. The government declared workers' intervention in management affairs to be unIslamic. Islamic societies were formed and began to intervene in the affairs of the *shoras* and to support the state-appointed managers. The workers faced the danger of losing all their revolutionary gains and being thrown back to where they had started. In protest, Shoraye Moassesse Ettehadieh Sarasariehe Karegarane Iran (the Founding Council of Iranian Workers Union throughout the Country) was formed to strengthen the individual *shoras* and to establish unity between them. On 1 March 1979, this body published a 24-point demand, including basic rights of workers to better wages and conditions, and trade union recognition. Following this, Ayatollah Khomeini, who for a long time had not publicly expressed any views about the *shoras*, made a speech asking the workers to trust the Islamic societies (which replaced the *shoras*) to save Iran from capitalism, imperialism and communism (Bayat 1987: 102–12; Poya 1987: 143–9).

During this period I was engaged in trade union activities with women industrial workers in four factories: Serum Sazi (vaccine making), Squibb (both part of the pharmaceuticals industry), Minoo biscuit factory and Gherghereh Ziba in the textile industry. A woman friend and I helped these women in their struggles within the *shoras*, the weakening of which was particularly damaging to female workers. For example, the *shoras* played an important role in setting up workplace nurseries, allowing women to continue to work outside the home without worrying about their children being left alone or in the streets. Zahra, a member of Serum Sazi's *shora*, explained at the time:

> The most important problem for women workers in this factory, like everywhere else, is the child-care problem. Most women leave their jobs

when they become pregnant. Some will come back to work when their babies are older. They usually leave their children with their family, relatives or even sometimes with neighbours. Most women workers are either young women who are not married or do not have children, or are middle-aged women whose children are grown up. One of our demands is, therefore, a workplace nursery, which we pushed through the *shora* and we won the battle with the management. The management has agreed to build a nursery, but they said that the *shora* is responsible for finding appropriate land near the factory. We considered this a way to put us off, but we are actively looking for appropriate land.

The setting up of literacy classes was also important because illiterate women were automatically categorised as unskilled, low-paid workers. Fatemeh from Squibb factory explained:

Equal pay legislation operates in this factory. Women are supposed to be paid equal to men for doing the same job, but in the majority of cases the lower educational status of women prevents them obtaining equal wages. For example, men and women work with machines, but only those who are literate get extra payment. There is more illiteracy among women. So in reality equal wage for doing an equal job does not exist. That is why we are demanding literacy classes for the illiterates.

Particularly important for female workers were health issues, such as the use of chemicals in the pharmaceuticals industry or the harsh conditions of work in the textiles industry, which were dangerous to the reproductive system. Zahra from Serum Sazi explained:

Conditions are still very harsh. The air is extremely polluted with chemicals. There is no proper ventilation. Most workers suffer from weak eyesight, chest problems and skin diseases. We need a *shora* to push for proper ventilation, masks and spectacles to protect us. We need showers and sinks to wash the chemicals off our faces, hands and bodies. There is only one shower and one sink in the whole factory, which is not enough. There is never any soap. We hardly use the shower because we are not allowed to use it within working hours; if we do, we have to work extra hours in order to cover for the time that we spend in the shower. The majority of workers in this factory are women, and the effect of chemicals on women is worse than on men, because if they are pregnant or if they breast-feed they suffer more and they transfer the chemicals to their babies.

In this period women's trade union activities also raised gender consciousness. For the first time these women were engaged in independent trade union activities as women. This was significant in a number of ways: the *shoras* were under attack from the Islamic state. Both female and male workers were struggling to save the *shoras*. But male workers were against female representation. They believed that women should leave these activities to men. For their part, women believed that they should be represented in the *shoras* as women workers, because they had specific demands. Zahra from Serum Sazi explained:

> In this factory 60 per cent of the workers are women. After the revolution, men workers could not ignore us, as our numbers were greater than theirs. They could not exclude us from the *shoras*. We managed to have four women representing 60 per cent of the workers and eleven men representing 40 per cent of the workers.

And Mehri from Gherghereh Ziba explained:

> After the revolution we wanted to create our *shora*. We elected a committee, the meeting was nearly ending and there was no talk about women's participation in the *shora* and their representation. Suddenly one of the women from the back of the hall shouted 'women should also be in the *shora*, we have to have our own representatives'. There was a lot of disagreement from the men; they argued that this is not women's business, it is bad for women to engage themselves in these affairs. This means women following the men's path. Women argued that if it is not bad to follow your path into work every day, how can it be bad for us to speak for ourselves and defend our rights? Finally, after a lot of argument, five men and two women were elected as representatives of the *shora*.

After a few months the Islamic state began consolidating its power through Islamisation of the whole of society. Islamic societies replaced all independent organisations, including the *shoras*. Strikes and sit-ins were labelled 'communist and imperialist conspiracies' and were attacked by armed police. It was no longer possible for us to continue to work with these women. However, this period was important for women workers and activists. These struggles delayed the Islamic state monopolising its power and consolidating its autocratic rule. This allowed women workers and activists to participate in political struggle, the experience of which was extremely important, and useful to them at a later stage. Despite Islamisation, the struggle for trade unionism continued. When I interviewed four of

these women in 1989, after ten years, I learned that they were still
within the Islamic Societies fighting for better working conditions.
Badri from Gherghereh Ziba explained:

> Conditions are still very hard. The majority of women work on the
> morning shift, which is from 6 a.m. to 2 p.m. We have only fifteen
> minutes' breakfast time, when they give us one potato, a bowl of beans
> and a piece of bread. We have to eat our breakfast next to our machine,
> which will be switched on when the fifteen-minute break is over. The
> air is very polluted. Bits of cottons hang in the air; sometimes we feel
> as though we have swallowed about a kilogramme of cotton with our
> breakfast. We have been demanding for a long time to be given more
> time and a canteen to eat our breakfast, but the Islamic Societies have
> been ignoring our demands. We also suffer from noise and injury to
> our eyesight and fingers. The machines are very noisy and we must keep
> our eyes open all the time and look at every individual thread very
> carefully, so that they don't get entangled with each other, and at the
> same time we must clean each individual buckle. This makes our eyes
> red and weak and injures our fingers. We have therefore been demand-
> ing that under such hard conditions of work, we should at least have a
> lunch break, as we get up at 4 a.m. to be able to be at work by 6 a.m.
> and by the time we get home it is 4 p.m. All we have had to eat is a
> potato, a bowl of beans and a piece of bread. So far we have not been
> successful in our demands but we are trying and we will not give up.

Islamic societies gradually became the political voice of the conservative Islamists within workplaces, and they ceased operating as
trade union organisations. However, there are trade syndicates, which
are not totally independent of the state and the employers; their
responsibilities are to look after their members in different industries and services. In the 1990s, for the first time in Iran, a woman
was elected leader of the hairdressers' syndicate. This was for a
number of reasons. As discussed in Chapter 4, in some instances sex
segregation created space for women to hold important positions.
Also there are more female hairdressers than male, and these women
would not have allowed a man to represent them. This is one of the
biggest syndicates, having 991 members in Tehran alone. Afsarmolok
Yasan's responsibility is to look after the interests of her members
and to deal with health issues in relation to this public service.

For women workers, the revolution was an instrument by means
of which they could struggle to change and improve their conditions
of work. These women, by fighting for their specific demands,

learned through their collective experience that women's rights could only be achieved through their own participation and representation. Furthermore, they learned that they do not have to be submissive to their menfolk in order to improve their status.

Women's Political Response to the Islamic State

In April 1979 a referendum decided that Iran was to be an Islamic Republic under the leadership of Ayatollah Khomeini. Women's response to the Islamic state differed according to their socio-economic status and level of religious observance. Why did secular women wage a political campaign against the Islamisation of the state, and why did religious women welcome and support it?

Secular women's response

During and after the revolution, various women's organisations were formed. Each published their own literature and campaigned for women's rights: Ettehade Melli Zanan (National Union of Women)[1] produced a paper, Barabari (Equality), and later a magazine, Zanan Dar Mobareze (Women in Struggle). Anjomane Rahaie Zan (the Emancipation of Women Society) was the women's organisation of Communist Unity. It produced a paper, Rahaie Zan (Emancipation of Women). Jamiate Bidarie Zan (the Awakening of Women Society) was formed by women members of a pro-China political Organisation. It produced a paper, Bidarie Zan (Woman's Awakening). Jamiate Zanane Mobarez (Militant Women Society) was the women's organisation of the Union of Iranian Communists, which also had its paper, Zanane Mobarez (Militant Women). Etehade Enghelabie Zanane Mobarez (Revolutionary Unity of Militant Women) was the women's organisation of the Maoist Communist Party of Workers and Peasants, and its paper was Sepideh Sorkh (The Red Dawn) (Tabari and Yeganeh 1982: 201–29).

There was a similarity between these women's organisations and those of the 1940s–1960s, as they were sister organisations of various Marxist groups. A great celebration was prepared for 8 March 1979, after so many years of repression in the Shah's patriarchal state. However, it was on the eve of this celebration that Ayatollah Khomeini announced that women must wear hejabe eslami. In response to such a proclamation, hundreds of thousands of women who had been preparing to celebrate International Women's Day understood that they had to turn it into a day of action against the regime. Mass meetings were organised in girls' schools, colleges and Tehran University against Khomeini's Islamic laws. The demonstrators marched in the streets of Tehran to the Ministry of Justice and the Prime Minister's office and shouted the slogans: 'In the dawn of freedom, we already lack freedom'; 'Down with dictatorship'; 'We gave our lives for freedom, and we will fight again'. The *Hezbollahi* men attacked the demonstrators with stones, shouting: 'Our belief is not your belief. Get lost communists'; 'Either you put a scarf on your heads or we hit you on the head'; 'Either *hejab* or *tisab* [acid]'. This was the first mass demonstration of secular women after the revolution. They marched, without wearing the *chador*, against Ayatollah Khomeini and not the Shah. For a whole week there were further protest meetings and demonstrations against the Islamic state's anti-women legislation.

To undermine this impressive movement the clergy encouraged and organised religious women's counter-demonstrations. The state portrayed the demonstration of a large number of women wearing the black *chador* as Islamic women fighting (like Zaynab) alongside their brothers in the war against the enemies of Islam. These women marched confidently, rejuvenated and glorified by Islamic values. They condemned the secular women's demonstrations as anti-Islamic. They supported the Islamic political system without questioning the clergy's rules and regulations, which were imposing social control and depriving all women of their most elementary rights. These women were excited and moved not just by their belief in Islam but also by their involvement in political activities acknowledged and supported by the state. In the view of secular women, the Islamic state exploited the participation of these religious women as an effective way to crush the movement struggling against the seclusion of women within the home. In the eyes of religious women, the Islamic state provided measures for their empowerment; they were out of their seclusion in the home and their male kin had no objection to their marching and demonstrating for Islam and Ayatollah Khomeini. The Islamic state successfully exploited these women and instituted further attacks on women's rights.

In order to mount an effective campaign against Ayatollah Khomeini, many organisations and individual secular feminists agreed
that a united women's movement had to be built. As a result Shoraye
Hambastegie Zanan (the Women's Solidarity Council) was formed.
Beside these organisations, many women formed groups in offices
and workplaces and worked with the United Council. Whatever the
women's political orientations, they all saw the need to build their
own organisations and, regardless of their political differences, to
unite against the Islamic state's attack on women's rights.

Other organisations were set up to support the Islamic state:
Tashkilate Democratike Zanane Iran (Democratic Association of
Iranian Women), the Tudeh Party's women's organisation; Zanane
Tarafdare Nehzate Azadie Iran (Women Adherents of Freedom Movement of Iran); Sazemane Zanane Jebhe Melli (Women's Organisation
of National Front). There was also Jamiate Zanane Enghelabe Eslami
(Women's Society of Islamic Revolution), which was not a secular
organisation. But some women within these organisations also
supported the Council's activities and the independent women's
movement. Although they supported Khomeini's leadership and the
formation of the Islamic state, they felt that women's rights were
under threat and had to be fought for.

The women who were active in the independent women's movement were predominantly secular and worked as teachers, nurses,
students, lawyers, writers and office workers. But they also supported
the activities of female industrial workers in factories, setting up
workplace nurseries and organising for women's participation in the
election of workers' shoras. They also tried to engage women with
the general issues and activities of the Women's Solidarity Council.
Some went to Kurdistan, or to other parts of Iran where national
minorities are concentrated, to fight against the central government.

The Council embarked on a long campaign of joint activities to
culminate in a day of action on 25 November 1979. This period was
critical for the Islamic state. Many women were in opposition. Factories were occupied by workers. Demonstrations and meetings of
the unemployed were taking place all over the country. Peasants
were seizing land and were constantly fighting the regime's Revolutionary Guards. The war between the national minorities and the
central government was reaching its highest stage. The Islamic regime

was divided, and the fight for power within different factions was intensifying. It was at this point that the regime adopted its anti-imperialist slogans and activities. This was a successful strategy to undermine the opposition and to unite different forces under the Islamic state and Khomeini's leadership.

An anti-imperialist demonstration around the occupation of the United States' embassy was organised for 25 November 1979, the same day as the Women's Solidarity Council's day of action. The male-dominated leadership of the secular opposition argued that the women's day of action had to be called off. The Fedayeen Organisation, the biggest on the left, withdrew its support from the women's day of action and joined the regime's demonstration. Despite this defection, many women members of the Fedayeen's women's organisation supported the Women's Solidarity Council's activities, and the conference went ahead in Tehran Polytechnic. In an attempt to stop the conference, Islamic Guards cut off the electricity supply, but the conference was held successfully by candle-light. It condemned the measures taken by the regime against women and passed resolutions for further activities.

Meanwhile the Constitution was ratified, *Sharia* law replaced civil law, and women were denied the reforms they had gained under the Pahlavi (Paidar 1995: 256–62). In March 1980 the Women's Solidarity Council organised to celebrate International Women's Day on 8 March. The Fedayeen's women's organisation withdrew its support for women's day in order to disassociate itself from the Solidarity Council, which was known as a major force against Islamisation. It held a separate rally on International Women's Day, and this was the beginning of the end of the Women's Solidarity Council as an effective independent movement. On 6 May, Ayatollah Khomeini made his speech declaring that day, his own and Fatimah's birthday, to be Women's Day in Iran.

In July 1980, after several months of bitter struggle by secular women, the wearing of the Islamic *hejab* became compulsory. For the older generation, especially those involved in the women's movement of the 1930s–1950s, this brought back memories of the dictatorial Reza Shah Pahlavi, who forced women to take their *chadors* off in 1936. In both cases the state implemented its policy by force, as large sections of the population opposed its compulsory nature.

In the 1930s even secular women who were in favour of modern political and economic development were reluctant to take off their *chadors* and wear western-style hats. In 1979–81, even religious women who sympathised with the Islamic state opposed the violent way the policy was implemented. Women's groups and organisations demonstrated once again in front of the president's office. Thousands of women were attacked by religious fanatics using knives, clubs and stones.

In Squibb pharmaceuticals factory, where I was involved with women in the establishment of the *shora*, only 20 per cent wore the *chador*. When the wearing of *hejab* became compulsory, all, including the *chadori* women, protested and demonstrated outside the factory, demanding that it be voluntary.

By mid-1981, all political organisations, women's organisations and workers' organisations had been banned and ceased to exist. There are no statistics available, but it was widely believed that half the political prisoners were women, the only form of equality given to women in the Islamic state. Women were raped in jail and this was justified by the Islamic law of temporary marriage. One family told me that they received the news of their 17-year-old daughter's execution when a member of the Revolutionary Guards returned her belongings and gave the parents 600 Rials (equivalent to £3 in 1980). The guard explained that the Islamic state's policy was not to execute virgins, because if a woman dies a virgin she will go to heaven. Because the young woman acted against the Islamic state, she did not deserve to go to heaven. Therefore one of the guards temporarily married her the night before her execution and the money was the price for the temporary marriage.

For many secular women, the Pahlavi period, with all its limitations, had opened up opportunities to struggle to achieve a degree of autonomy in decision-making about their sexuality, fertility, earning and expenditure. This was observed and understood by many religious women, who also began to question their own status and what they might be able to achieve, if they risked breaking the rules. Azar, one of my respondents, confirmed this view:

> My parents were insisting that I should marry, as it was a disgrace for them that I was 20 years of age and unmarried. But I resisted, I did not want to be married. They did not force my brother to marry, who lived

with his Iranian girlfriend in London. I wanted to be independent, earn my own money, go and see the world and then marry, if I wanted to.

As a result of Islamisation many secular women chose to live in exile. Alma explained:

> I felt I was nothing but a subhuman in that society. The Islamic state in Iran was founded on sexual apartheid as well as dictatorship and repression. Under this system of apartheid, women were directly segregated and secluded by the laws of the state. There was no way out. This regime was about absolute control over the female body and mind. Women were limited to the rights, roles and tasks that the state saw fit for them. (Poya 1992: 159)

Many of these exiled women benefited from the socio-economic changes of the Pahlavi period. Despite this, many of them participated in the 1978–79 movements, and played an important role in the overthrow of that system. They therefore felt, and still feel, betrayed by the Islamic system that has replaced it (Poya 1992), especially when they see a large number of women participating in the reproduction of this Islamic patriarchal order. Now they use their academic work and their activities in campaigns for women's rights as a way of struggling with the patriarchal system in Iran by drawing the attention of world public opinion to women's position there.

Religious women's response

It is important to analyse the reasons why religious women found the Islamic state liberating, and how the state engaged them in organised political activities within the Islamic framework. After the 1979 revolution and the establishment of the Islamic state, a large number of women, some deprived and others from more privileged sectors of society, were attracted to the Islamic system. Under the Pahlavi they had experienced nothing but humiliation, because of their commitment to Islamic values. They had felt marginalised because they were ideologically and materially debased, degraded and neglected. The Pahlavi state ideologically restricted their access to secular education and employment. Therefore they did not benefit from the modern socio-economic system, which undermined some aspects of patriarchal gender relations. On the contrary, it was threatening to them. The state considered them backward if they did not give up their religious values and norms, and their male kin prohibited them from participating in changes which required such an abandonment. Hence they envied and detested those who benefited from the changes and adopted a western lifestyle. The Islamic regime exploited such sentiments and won these women to its side. They became staunch supporters of the Islamic regime. The regime declared them the guardians of Islamic society and the upholders of new morality and values. They became the symbol of Islamic womanhood. The Islamic state and its hegemonic ideology gave them access to material and ideological resources and provided them with a space to exercise power. Thus these women willingly participated in the making of this patriarchal system, which enhanced their sense of control and self-worth.

The secularists see these women as actively reproducing the patriarchal order (Hendessi and Shafii 1995: 12–15; Afshar 1994: 15–20). But for religious women, this patriarchal order has opened up opportunities for them to move out of the home and become engaged in positions of power as activists in the Islamic system.

In the 1980s, many were voluntary workers for Islamic organisations. This brought them prestige. Some worked because of religious commitment, others to promote the ideology of the Islamic state nationally and internationally. Larger numbers, however, worked for financial reasons; they were not paid a wage, but they were subsidised by the state. For example, they were rewarded with free accommodation from the houses confiscated from those who fled the country, and given extra rations, which they sold on the black market so as to earn a living.[2] These women were committed to the Islamic state and did not question its philosophy of the woman's place being in the home. However, their political activities in the revolutionary period and their paid and unpaid work in the 1980s gave them a sense of collective consciousness against their limited role in the home. Azam Taleghani, a member of the *Majles* in 1979–81, explained how women's experiences of voluntary work politicised them:

> During the war we joined the Baaseej Khaharan organisation. We worked in the mosques, prepared food, blankets and medicines for the men at the war front. In the war-zone areas, such as Ghasre Shirin, Bakhtaran and Sare Paule Zahab, women were involved in the distribution of arms

amongst the population and the soldiers. In these areas women set up mobile hospitals and looked after the injured. As the war continued, women had to return to their homes, but they still continued their voluntary work and had to organise their time in a way to allow them to do their housework and their voluntary work in order to keep male family members happy.

During this period, Taleghani's organisation, the Women's Society of Islamic Revolution, voluntarily taught women sewing, knitting and electronics work. This allowed them to be employed in textile and electronics industries. The organisation also ran classes in mathematics and Farsi for poorer students who needed help with their studies. Forough described her voluntary activities during the war with Iraq:

> During the war we became active once again. We went to demonstrations, meetings and conferences. My husband couldn't disagree; it was all for God. I took the children with me or left them with other women in the neighbourhood who agreed to look after the children while others went to these activities. We made trips to the Beheshte Zahra cemetery to comfort those who had lost their sons, husbands or fathers in the war. We helped the refugees from the war zone areas, and in the mosques we cooked food and canned it and we made blankets and clothes.

Despite a fall in their number by 1991, there was still a significant body of women who worked on a voluntary basis for the Islamic organisations. Most of these, however, had no children or their children were grown up. I asked one active member of the literacy crusade the reason for her activities. She replied:

> I teach in Isfahan [central Iran] in the morning and I fly to Mashahd [Eastern Iran] in the evening, teaching Quran and religious education. I do it for God, I hope that God will accept my services, as I feel that I am not doing enough for him. However, if my husband does not agree, God will not agree either, therefore I will stop my activities the moment he asks me to.

The Islamic state provided material and ideological opportunities for religious women to exercise a degree of power, in comparison with their status under the Pahlavi. But by emphasising women's place in the home, the state ignored varied women's responses and intensified the patriarchal relationship. It used Fatimah and Zaynab as symbols to legitimise the political participation of women, and thereby politically benefited from women's participation in support of the Islamic state. Nevertheless, their activism and their participation in work raised their gender consciousness, and they began to question the limitations of the state's gender ideology. This created conflict within the family and the wider society, and, in the 1990s, women began to question the differential treatment advocated by the state. Although in the 1980s religious and secular women were a world apart, by the 1990s a form of unity had come about, despite social differentiation, through identification of similar problems and experiences. I shall focus on women's activism through the media and in politics which forced the Islamic state towards pragmatism.

Media

In March 1998 a women's publishers' book exhibition demonstrated how a large number of women use the media. An impressive forty-seven women publishers,[3] five women's organisations,[4] Alzahra women's university and seven women's newspapers and magazines[5] exhibited their publications. Shahla Lahiji, who in the early 1990s established the first women's publishing house in Iran, Entesharate Roshangaran (The Enlighteners), said in her concluding remarks about the success of the exhibition: 'Maybe in one hundred years from today many more women publishers will get together and remember us and our efforts as the first women publishers in Iran.'[6] By 1999 the number of women publishers had increased to 236.

The film industry in Iran in the 1990s has opened up opportunities for female film directors and actors to discuss gender relations. Prior to 1979 there were only two female directors in Iran.[7] By the late 1990s there were at least ten,[8] and the emphasis had moved away from ghostly images of women in the background or in a domestic environment to a portrayal of women as virtuous, active and socially constructive (Nafisy 1994). These films explicitly criticised patriarchal relationships under the Islamic state, and at the same time conveyed a strong message that women, as active participants in social issues, are in a position to change society.[9] Outside Iran, Iranian secular women film-makers are also echoing how women in Iran fight by any means necessary for their rights, and force men and the male-dominated society to listen to their voice and, more importantly, win.[10]

By 1999 there were at least ten[11] women's newspapers, magazines and journals actively discussing women's issues, ranging from debates over feminism and patriarchy to women's position within the family, employment, law and education. They also represented different forms of Muslim feminism in Iran. For example, women active around *Payame Zan* magazine limit their activities to interpreting the Quran and *hadith* (collected sayings of the prophet Mohammad) in ways complementary to women's issues. *Zane Rouz* and *Payame Hajar* have gone further, criticising laws and regulations that are detrimental to women, and suggesting reforms. *Zanan* has questioned gender relations through an analysis of women's issues in Islam and different feminist schools of thought. *Farzaneh* has devoted its pages to researching feminist issues in Iran and elsewhere, and has made contacts with feminist organisations around the world (Tohidi 1996: 279–6).

In 1998, five other women's magazines and newspapers (*Mahtab*, *Neda*, *Kokab*, *Hoghoghe Zanan* and *Rouznameh Zan*) were added to this list. The publication of *Hoghoghe Zanan* has drawn attention to the question of violence against women. Publication of the daily *Rouznameh Zan* by Faezeh Hashemi in August 1998 was an important step towards relating women's issues to a growing democracy movement, on the basis of day-to-day political struggle for the establishment of a civil society in Iran. In April 1999 this newspaper was closed down for challenging the *ghessas* law: it published a cartoon showing a gunman attempting to kill a man and a woman; the male victim makes an appeal to him, saying, 'Don't kill me, kill her as she is cheaper.'

Women's issues became central within Iranian politics. This process began in the early 1990s, when magazines, newspapers, television and radio raised these issues with women's participation. The powerful presence of religious Iranian women, wearing black *chador*, as delegates to the International Women's Conference in Bejing in 1995 brought to the fore gender issues in Iran. Many secular Iranian women exiled abroad also attended the conference. Their interaction raised many questions in relation to women's economic, social and political roles in Iran. Many important issues relating to women's role in education, employment and population control were raised and led to heated debates in the Iranian media about inequalities between women and men in Islamic Iran. For example, *Payame Emrouz* (Today's Message), a monthly economic, social and cultural magazine, wrote: 'Women are half of the population but only a small percentage of them are employed or self-employed. Their activities are mainly concentrated in domestic work. National development would be impossible without women's economic participation' (*Payame Emrouz* No. 8, 1995). In opposition to this view, *Sobh* (Morning) weekly newspaper wrote: 'Even if we accept that women's presence in economic activities is necessary we must make sure that women's priority is in the home' (*Sobh* No. 26, 1995). The female chief editor of *Maiyar* (Criterion) monthly magazine and the author of an article, 'Would you have been in this position, if you were a woman?', based on interviewing a number of men in high positions, concluded that the ideology of women's priority being the home was an obstacle to their upward mobility (*Maiyar* No. 15, 1995).

Women's magazines and journals have played an important role as a forum for the views of both religious and secular women. These publications, although they were set up by religious women and supporters of the Islamic state, decided to seek a wider audience by inviting secular women to contribute to the debate on women's issues. For example, Shahla Shirkat, editor of *Zanan*, suggested that 'we should tolerate and respect each others' conviction. Even though we do not share the same philosophy, belief and thought, we can and should work together' (Kian 1997: 91). In the 1980s, Mahbobeh Abbas-Gholizadeh (Ommi) wrote a number of articles in *Zane Rouz* rejecting feminism, especially the notion of Muslim feminism in Iran. In the 1990s, however, she changed her position and, as the editor of *Farzaneh*, argued that women's issues and feminism must be studied systematically, her aim in *Farzaneh* being to do just this (Tohidi 1996: 279–80). The aim of these Muslim feminists has been to put pressure on the Islamic state by emphasising that inequalities between men and women do not originate in the Quran, but rather in the interpretation by religious authorities of the divine laws. By taking this position they have succeeded in forcing the state to reform family laws, employment legislation and constitutional law.

During the parliamentary elections in 1996 and the presidential election in 1997, *Zanan* magazine published different views by women on women's demands for reforms of family law, female education and employment regulations, and in the summer of 1997, in a series of articles in the form of a round-table, discussed the question, 'What is the most important problem facing women in Iran?' The magazine also sent the following questions to be discussed at a round-table at the 1997 International Conference on Middle Eastern Studies at the University of Oxford in Britain:

1. What was the most important problem facing women in Iran? If there was a list of burning issues, what issues came top of the list?
2. Having defined what the problems were, how far were they related to the wider political context and how far to the position of women?
3. Do women in Iran have a problem which unites them all?. If so, how much are these problems related specifically to the Iranian context and how much to the universal context?
4. What is the root problem?

Because of the breadth of this agenda and time constraints, the participants, including Kaar, a woman lawyer from Iran, decided to focus on the important issue of women's political participation and the struggles of women to seek formal political influence within the legislature. Kaar emphasised that in the 1990s both secular and Muslim feminists in Iran rejected institutionalised inequalities and increasingly demanded further changes. More importantly, she argued that the legal reform which had taken place was the result of women's activities inside and outside the country and that the changes are irreversible. This discussion raised the issue of whether women's demands in Iran were 'feminist issues'. Kaar explained that they might be feminist demands within the global context, but not in the Iranian context. Under the Islamic state such labels were not used. These issues were, however, debated and discussed as part of the issue of human equality.

In August 1998, during the election of *Majles Khebregan* (the Assembly of Experts), Faezeh Hashemi published the daily *Rouznameh Zan* (Women's Newspaper). This newspaper, with a circulation of twenty thousand, waged a campaign to include women in the assembly, and encouraged women to stand for election. The writers argued that even if women were not elected, their participation would give them the necessary confidence to participate in future, and would draw the attention of the authorities to the importance of women's active role in politics (31 August 1998). They also argued that this assembly could not be the sphere of the clergy alone, but must include women knowledgeable in religious, political, cultural and managerial issues (9 September 98). As a result of this campaign, 10 women stood for election for the first time with 386 men, but they were rejected, because, according to the Islamic constitution, women cannot be included in such an assembly (20 September 1998).

The importance of the media in expressing women's activism is also evident in the increasing number of female journalists in Iran. Despite the great restrictions imposed on them by segregation, in the 1990s there are far more female journalists in Iran than there were in the 1970s, the height of westernisation and the reforms of the Pahlavi state (Farhadpour 1998). In 1972 there were two thousand journalists in Iran, and only fifty of them (2.5 per cent) were women. In 1997 there were four thousand journalists, of whom four hundred (10 per cent) were women. Iranian women journalists are on average five years younger than their male colleagues, but they are considerably better educated – 50 per cent are graduates, while the average for the entire profession is 35 per cent (Shahidi 1997). This was facilitated by Muslim feminists in positions of power. Shahla Habibi, adviser on women's issues under President Rafsanjani argued:

> We need more reporters, producers and directors with expertise on women's issues. Just as economics needs to be covered by a journalist who knows about economics, journalists covering women's issues should be aware of women's mentality, language, literature, and their desirable status from the point of view of religion and tradition ... journalists have to be educated about women's issues, and special women's groups have to be set up within the various media organisations. (Shahidi 1997)

As a result of women's active participation in the media, in 1998, for the first time in the modern history of Iran, a women journalists' trade association, Anjomane Senfieh Rouzname Negaran Zan, was formed. This could be a step towards the establishment of genuine trade unions in Iran, within a growing democracy movement and creation of civil society.

Politics

From the onset of the Islamic state until the 1996 presidential election, no form of secularism was tolerated. Secular organisations did not exist; Islamic political parties and organisations expressed different opinions about economic, political, social and foreign affairs. Within strict bounds, universal suffrage and freedom of speech, press and assembly obtained. Many people felt that they were participating in political life, eagerly following debates in the *Majles*, the judicial system and the government through the media. This form of Islamic pluralism and parliamentary rule was different from the autocratic state of the Pahlavi, in which no opposition was tolerated, even within the ruling class. The Islamic state had no choice but to accommodate this limited pluralist system. The 1979 revolution, which overthrew the Pahlavi system, and the impact of the various movements which opposed the establishment of the Islamic state were not forgotten, and the majority of the people actively demanded democratic change. This was evident when President Khatami won a landslide victory in the 1996 presidential election and for the first time since the establishment of the Islamic state, Nehzate Azadi (Liberation movement), a secular liberal organisation, became active, including publication of a magazine *Iran Farda* (Tomorrow's Iran).

During the period 1998–99 the constant demands of the majority of the population led to a democracy movement and a bitter power struggle with the conservative clergy and their supporters, now in the minority within the political institutions and rapidly losing popular support. During this political power struggle, a number of writers, poets and political activists were murdered in terrorist attacks by conservative elements – among them Parvaneh Eskandari Forouhar, a well-known political activist. Newspapers, journals and magazines were closed down; editors, journalists and proprietors were arrested and tortured. Nevertheless the democracy movement went from strength to strength. As a result, the arrested were released and banned publications reopened. For example, *Jameah* (Society) newspaper, at the forefront of the democracy movement, was reopened under the name of *Tous*; it then closed down and reopened again under the name of *Neshat*. More importantly, in early 1999 Kanoone Nevisandegan Iran (The Writers' Association of Iran), a secular organisation of hundreds of writers ranging from Marxists to liberals, began its political activity in response to the growing democracy movement by distributing leaflets, pamphlets and open letters to state institutions demanding reforms.

The role of women in this process has been significant. They have been active in the political arena, on gender issues, as voters and as elected members of the *Majles*. In the parliamentary election of April 1996 and the presidential election of May 1997, women's participation showed that gender had become an important force shaping politics in Islamic Iran. One important feature of the election in 1996 was that 190 women competed with 3,010 men for 270 seats. As was widely reported in the media, especially women's magazines, the majority of women voted for female candidates, on the ground that only women could change women's situation. Even in conservative regions (Isfahan and Malayer), women competed with men – in some cases with the clergy – winning either the election or a large number of votes (*Keyhan* 28 March 1996; *Iran Focus*, February–April 1996).

In 1996 I interviewed a number of men and women about this matter. There were at least three different explanations. For example, a middle-aged man from Malayer who voted for the female candidate said that he voted for that *zaifeh* (the weak half) because 'her programme was better than others'. A young woman's response was that 'only women can do things for women'. And an older woman's response was 'women are less corrupt and work better when they get to positions of power'. Women's issues and the question of female candidates were debated within family circles. Faezeh Hashemi, who stood in Tehran against the prominent conservative cleric Nateghe Nouri, became extremely popular among young women of both the religious and the secular middle class for suggesting that if elected she would create women-only sport grounds, including horseriding and women-only cycle lanes. Not only did religious women vote for her, but secular women also, despite the fact that she was the daughter of a clergyman (ex-president Rafsanjani). In the election she came second. It was widely believed that the count was rigged, as it would have been embarrassing to the Islamic state for a young women to beat a prominent clergyman. Nevertheless thirteen women were elected to the *Majles*.[12]

In the 1997 presidential election, women's issues were once again at the centre of political debates. Despite the fact that, according to religious law and Article 115 of the Constitution, women could not become president, nine women stood (*Iran Focus* May–June 1997;

Payame Emrouz No. 19, 1997; *Zanan* No. 34, 1997). This action was a form of protest, forcing the state to admit to its own limitations. This was explained by one of the candidates, Azam Taleghani, the head of the Women's Society of Islamic Revolution and editor of the women's newspaper *Payame Hajar*. She announced that her intention was first 'to sort out the interpretation of the term *rejal* (statesman)', which is ambiguously defined in the Constitution; second, she said, 'It was my religious duty to stand for the presidential election, otherwise the rights of half of the population of this country would have been wasted and I would have been responsible and account-able to God for such an injustice.' Third, she explained, 'I have discussed with a number of clergymen the issue of whether a woman could be the president of the Islamic Republic or not in order to pave the way for the future, even if this may cause problems for me at present' (*Payame Emrouz* No. 19, 1997; *Zanan* No. 34, 1997).

Despite these attempts, all female applicants were rejected by *Shoraye Negahban* (the Council of Guardians). But women's issues were still at the heart of the debate. *Zanan* magazine asked a number of questions of Khatami (the pragmatic candidate) and Nateghe Nouri (the conservative candidate, who had competed with Faezeh Hashemi in the 1996 parliamentary election) about their views on women's issues. Khatami's answers were sympathetic, but Nateghe Nouri refused to answer. The magazine also interviewed a number of women in academic, artistic, political and scientific positions about their demands from the candidates (*Zanan* No. 34, 1997).

As a result of these campaigns, the majority of women and youth (especially young women) voted for Khatami, who won a landslide victory against Nateghe Nouri. Gender consciousness determined the outcome of the election. They voted for Khatami because they believed that under his presidency women's issues could be fought for more easily than under the conservative Nouri. It was expected that two women would be included in Khatami's cabinet: Fatemeh Ramezanzadeh, a *Majles* deputy and Iran's representative at the Cairo Population and Development Conference in 1994, was expected to be minister of health, and the popular Faezeh Hashemi was nominated to be minister of sport, a new ministry to be created for youth (*Iran Focus*, June 1997). However, in response to pressure from conservative clergy, President Khatami refused to include any women in his cabinet, which was formed in August 1997. But Masoomeh Ebtekar was included in the cabinet as vice-president, responsible for environmental issues, and Zahra Shojaie was appointed adviser to the president and the head of the Centre for Women's Participation.

In September 1998, *Rouznameh Zan* reported a nationwide opinion poll suggesting that 85 per cent of women in Iran follow political issues in the media, especially radio and television. Of those polled, 65 per cent demanded that President Khatami include at least three women ministers in his cabinet to deal with women's economic, political, social and cultural issues (2 September 1998).

The local council elections of early 1999 also saw women actively participating in politics as both voters and candidates. Women activists in the media and politics encouraged women's participation and officially asked local authorities to identify potential female candidates, to encourage women to stand and to facilitate their campaigns (*Zanan* No. 50, 1998). Many women candidates concentrated on the issues of democratic rights and the creation of civil society. Once again women's political participation resulted in the defeat of the conservatives and a landslide victory for the reformers. More importantly, many women were elected as local council members: women were elected in 25 provinces; in 109 cities women won the highest number of votes; 23 cities have at least one woman member, in 48 cities there are two women members, in 8 cities there are three women members, in the small city of Saveh there are four women, and in Konoug in the southeastern province of Kerman the entire village council is female (*Rouznameh Zan* 15 March 1999). This means that a large number of women will be participating in decision-making at both city and local levels in economic, political, social and cultural issues.

The existence of eighty-four women's organisations, including non-governmental organisations (NGOs), charities and cultural organisations (Zoroastrian, Jewish and Christian as well as Muslim) around the country is another measure of women's activities in different spheres.

In the first and the second phases of Islamisation (1979–89) the Islamic state isolated secular women and favoured the participation of only religious women, in the interest of the patriarchal state. In the third phase (1990s), however, especially in the 1996, 1998 and

1999 elections, and especially in urban areas, women participated in politics on a mass scale. This was because women, regardless of differences of class and faith, had experienced shared problems: Islamic family law enforced male domination in the family, at work and in the wider society, despite the fact that women generated income for their families and saved expenditure for the state. Religious women especially felt that although they had supported state patriarchy, their interests were ignored. This raised women's consciousness about the limitations of the state's gender ideology. Although the subordination of women was deeply ingrained in the consciousness of both men and women, women (and men) also saw from their own experiences that the state and the family benefited from women's participation in the spheres of economy and politics.

Moreover, these shared problems and experiences had closed the gap between religious women who supported the Islamic system and the secular women who opposed it. Both were aware that despite their economic and political participation, the institutionalisation of patriarchy had strengthened male domination and women's subordination. Both wanted changes to their circumstances, and they made the men and the state accept their participation and their demands.

In the Islamic state, where secularism is only beginning to be tolerated and secular organisations are beginning to operate openly, only Muslim feminists have access to the political sphere. Female political activists such as Shahla Habibi (daughter of Ayatollah Habibi), Fatimah and Faezeh Hashemi (daughters of ex-president Rafsanjani) and Azam Taleghani (daughter of the late Ayatollah Taleghani) have tried, within the Islamic state apparatus, to reinterpret Islamic laws and regulations in favour of women's participation in economics and politics. Many secular feminists in Iran feel that, although the real change should come from an end to state theocracy, these reforms are not in conflict with their demands for equal treatment within the family, in employment and generally. More importantly, the unity between secular and Muslim feminists has challenged Islamic theology and thereby the Iranian theocratic state, with the result that the state has been forced to adapt its ideological position and practices.

Women's Individual Responses

Besides organised struggle, the majority of women also struggle on an individual basis against patriarchal gender relations. This form of struggle is equally important because the forms of gender relations and women's subordination to men are not static, but change according to economic conditions. Any real change in women's subordination must come from changes in social relations rather than change in the law. Women's individual responses to patriarchal relationships could also, therefore, have great impact on the position of women. But these responses differ according to class and religious position.

Kandiyoti (1991: 35–8) argues that individual women interpret and reinterpret patriarchal ideology and use it as a form of struggle; women are not passive victims of ideology. This analysis is important because it explains why, in Iran, many women accept their subordinate position and some participate in the reproduction of their own subordination by policing the patriarchal state and its rules and regulations. For many women, involvement in policing the patriarchal state was the source of their empowerment. In this sense the ideology had a material basis, which women used to improve their status. Thus, acceptance of the ruling ideology was not just a result of false consciousness (Molyneux 1985: 227–54). In effect it was a way of bargaining with patriarchy.

If seclusion and segregation created constraints on women's mobility, which varied according to access to material resources and ideological position, women chose different strategies, sometimes rebelling against the stated gender ideology, at other times conforming to it. They chose these strategies to achieve a particular goal: to survive or to secure a better future and improve their economic and social status. Grown and Sebstad (1989: 941), in the context of analysing women's poverty and livelihood activities, identify three different goals: for the poorest, survival; for those whose basic survival is assured, their goal may shift to security – available resources allow a degree of flexibility and risk; finally, for those who have achieved basic security, the goal may change to growth. I use these concepts alongside Kandiyoti's concept of bargaining with patriarchy to analyse how women in Iran struggled on an individual basis against the conflicts arising from Islamic gender ideology and the material reality of their lives. Some observed Islamic rules; others rebelled. But most chose a mixed strategy to survive and improve their circumstances.

Breaking the Rules

According to official statistics, the female population of Iran in 1996/7 was 29,540,329, the male population 30,515,159. Of these women, 18,012,766 or 61 per cent lived in urban areas (Iran Statistical Yearbook 1996/7: 37). In urban areas women had better access to resources than rural women: the level of literacy and further and higher education was higher. Secular women had the option of not getting married, or marrying after they had completed their higher education. Many of these women resisted patriarchal gender relations by breaking the rules, even though they may have lost out on the family front. Unmarried and divorced women paid a heavy price for finding empowerment in a career and clinging to their independence from men, by losing their reputation or the custody of their children, but this was their way of bargaining with patriarchy. Their access to material resources, combined with being less constrained by the values of Shii Islam, enabled them to struggle against the conflicts and secure a better future or improve their status in their chosen way.

Single women had a greater degree of autonomy to make decisions about their sexuality, fertility, earnings and disposal of income. Even if they did not work out of economic necessity, they chose to have a career in order to be independent and upwardly mobile. However, the norm did not allow them to live on their own; hence they usually lived with their parents and chose to give them a portion of their earnings to guarantee their independence from them. Their motivation, despite Islamic gender ideology, was to improve their status, their place and power in comparison with men. Simin, a 33-year-old accountant identifying herself as middle class with low religious observance, explained:

> I have no intention of getting married. Segregation does not allow me to meet a suitable person. I cannot marry someone who is in a lower position in terms of education and employment. Men don't like women

who are in a higher position than themselves because this makes it harder for them to have control over women. I live with my parents to keep people's mouths shut. I work for the state sector in the morning and in a private company in the afternoon and evening. I leave the house at 7 a.m. and return home at 9 p.m. The state sector gives me the security and I earn a lot of money in the private sector.

Conforming to the Rules

Many religious women, especially those with limited access to material resources and waged employment, bargained with patriarchy by conforming to most of its rules. This was especially apparent in rural areas. In 1996/7 the female population of rural areas was 11,421,321 (Iran Statistical Yearbook 1996/7: 37). They were among the poorest and were most affected by gender inequality. The reform of the family law, education and employment regulations had not affected these women greatly. Despite education reform and rising literacy, 55 per cent of rural women were still illiterate (Iran Statistical Yearbook 1996/7: 514). They married young, usually in their mid-teens. They had high fertility. They started working on the land, or as carpet-weavers, when they were as young as 5 or 6 years old. Their work was important for the household, national and international markets. The majority of them, however, were not recorded in the statistics as part of the workforce.

Thus, the majority of female agricultural workers whose access to material resources was limited and who were constrained by gender ideology achieved their goal by conforming to the rules of separate spheres for women and men. This was a bargain with patriarchy because, as Kandiyoti argues, 'in situations where the observance of restrictive practices is a crucial element in the reproduction of family status, women will resist breaking the rules' (1991: 33). Under classic patriarchy, women accommodate to the system and 'their passive resistance takes the form of claiming their half of this particular patriarchal bargain – protection in exchange for submissiveness and propriety, and a confirmation that male honour is indeed dependent on their responsible conduct' (1991: 36).

The labour of these women had always been demanded, but it is secluded and segregated labour. In this sense they were not exposed to the same conflicts as women who were drawn into wage labour. They were aware of their contribution, but under the pressure of gender ideology they believed that decisions had to be made by men. The only time they participated in decision-making was in their old age, especially when their daughters got married. The preparation of *jahizieh* was the responsibility of women, especially older women. Ameh Khanom, a 57-year-old carpet-weaver and agricultural worker, the mother of eight children, explained:

> We have a good annual income from the production of grapes, cumin, barley, cotton, wheat, pistachios and carpet-weaving. These are mostly women's jobs, especially carpet-weaving. Boys up to the age of 10 weave carpets and then they go to school but girls remain carpet-weavers and work on the land. Women also produce milk, yoghurt, butter, cheese and bread. A large part of our income pays for raw materials, machinery and access to water. Men take the products to the market and sell them to government agents. We never go to the market, as this is men's job. My husband gives me a lot of money to prepare *jahizieh* for our daughters.

For Ameh Khanom, the most important issue was that she achieved her goal and ultimately gained power by conforming to what was expected of her. She was not simply submitting to her subordinate position; her survival and the survival of her family depend on her acceptance of her position.

The case of Akhtar, in a village in the north of Iran, was similar. She left school when she was 10 years old and continued carpet-weaving and working on the land. She married when she was 16. She followed her husband, who was a soldier, to Chahbahar in the south of Iran. She had four children. She also found survival and security through conforming to an ascribed role, although she was totally aware of her ability to earn money. She explained:

> I finish all the housework in the morning. I then spend the rest of my time knitting, sewing and doing embroidery. My husband sells them all. Every summer I come back to my village and weave carpets. In a good month I could earn up to 200,000 Rials. My husband sells the carpets. He is very happy with me and appreciates my work.

In these cases women were outside waged employment. But even in the case of industrial workers in a margarine factory, a similar form of patriarchal bargain was evident. These women, although wage-earners, could not build on their experience of waged labour as a means to challenge patriarchy. Their strategy was to secure honour and pride for their families and community by refusing to use contraceptives until they produced sons, and they even attempted to give up their jobs in favour of their male kin, in order to gain respectability.

These women were actively participating in cultural negotiations to reinterpret the rules and regulations to their advantage, rather than passively accepting the patriarchal rule. They were, therefore, mobilising their material resources and ideological constraints in order to achieve their goals. Some were able to move from survival to security and others to move forward and improve their own and their families' status.

A Mix of Strategies

Those who rebelled against the patriarchal rules were a small minority. Those who conformed to the rules were a large minority. The majority of women, both in rural and urban areas, bargained with patriarchy by using a mixture of conformity and rebellion. Their degree of access to material resources and ideological constraint determined to what extent they conformed or rebelled and their ability to achieve a particular goal. In some cases, women took all the responsibility for domestic work to keep family and husband satisfied, and at the same time worked doubly hard in their profession to prove that they were as good as men. As a result, some women's daily hours of work increased up to seventeen hours. In other cases, as many of my interviewees pointed out, women had to deny their greater access to resources and mobility in order to maintain the honour of the husband and the family. They had to pretend to the members of their families and community that the husband was in charge; he was the breadwinner and the property and belongings were his. This is similar to the concept of 'sexual anomie' (Mernissi 1987: 148–53), where men are frustrated and humiliated at being unable to fulfil their role as breadwinner. In order to reduce tension and conflict, women bargained with patriarchy by denying their greater access to material resources because this was the only way they could gain respectability.

In rural areas, those women who had some access to material resources but were heavily constrained by gender ideology also attempted to achieve their goals by using a mix of strategies. For example, Maryam, who lived in a small village in Khorasan province, was not exposed to much economic hardship and insecurity compared with other women in the village. She had cousins and brothers in the big cities, who had set an example by exercising choice and thereby held out the possibility of change. From the moment that we arrived, Maryam tried hard to convince her cousin who lived in the city to negotiate with her father to allow her to leave the village and go to a nearby city to continue her education:

> I have been working as a carpet-weaver and agricultural worker since I was 10 years old. I have just finished primary school education this summer. It took me such a long time to achieve this level of education because during school-time I had to leave school and concentrate on working on the land and weaving carpets. I live with my father, step-mother (Zahra) and stepbrother. I have four brothers and three sisters who are all married and live in big cities. My father sells the carpets and the agricultural products that my stepmother and I produce. In return for the work that I do, my father prepares Jahizieh for me, clothes and household appliances for when I get married. I don't want to get married. I want to go to Kashmar and finish my education and later, hopefully, go to Tehran and work as a nurse. But my father will not allow me. He says if I go he has to hire labourers who will cost him a lot of money. Also if I go to the cities without being married people will talk and I'll be a disgrace to my father. One of my brothers lives in Kashmar. I could go and live with him and his family. This way people won't talk. I want to get my cousin to mediate; if he does, my father may agree.

This way, Maryam actively participated in cultural negotiations with her father, her extended family, and her community through her cousin. It was a risk for her but she succeeded. As a result of mediation she secured a better future for herself by leaving the village, moving to a city and continuing her education. The experience of one side of the family doing better by moving to the city was a contradiction for her and everyone else in the village. Our visit stirred up this contradiction. Maryam used the confusion, broke the rules and achieved her goal of securing a better future. However, she could rebel against one set of rules only by conforming to another. She had to accept being under the control of her brother in a city in order to be free of the control of her father in a village. Only in this way could she finish her education and work as a nurse, which was her goal.

Similarly, in a village in Mazandaran, Golrang, a carpet-weaver and agricultural worker, managed to continue her education, achieved a high-school diploma and began to work as a teacher in the village school. This allowed her to escape the pressure from her family to get married. She explained:

> I am unusual in the village in that I am 23 years old and have not been married yet, but there is no real pressure. My father and my mother agree with my work as a teacher. But I don't think the people in the village value my teaching job, because nobody ever says anything, while they value the carpets that I weave, because they talk about it. I continue with both and I like both jobs and I also help my mother and father with the agricultural production. My father sells the carpets that my mother, my sisters and I weave and also the agricultural products that we produce. But most of the time I keep my earnings from teaching. If my family need money, I give my salary to my father, but if they do not need it, I keep it for myself.

In this case Golrang was able to mobilise the ideological constraints to her advantage, in comparison with her sister Akhtar. On the one hand, she was conforming to the norm by working as an agricultural worker and a carpet-weaver and accepting the appropriation of her labour by her father. On the other hand, she took the opportunity of making a choice not to get married, continued her education, worked as a teacher, earned a wage and, most importantly, made decisions about whether to save her money or help her family with her earnings.

Thus, in the majority of cases, the strength of male authority in the family and at the level of the state did not allow much rebellion against the norm. As a way to survive poverty or to achieve a sense of righteousness and self-worth, conformity is more widespread than rebellion. However, further economic integration of Iran into the world market in the late 1980s and 1990s, a relative improvement in women's education and employment opportunities, and the reform of some aspects of family law have led to a further integration of material and ideological factors. As a result most women choose a mixture of conformity and rebellion in conflicts arising from material and ideological integration.

Women's individual responses against patriarchal relations formed a pattern that could be observed throughout society, and this, combined with different, organised, collective responses has increased gender consciousness and affected the state's gender relations.

Conclusion

In discussing women's political participation in Iran since the 1979 revolution, I have stressed the importance of their responses to patriarchal gender ideology in both organised and individual forms. Their responses varied according to their social class and degree of religious observance. The mass participation of women in the revolution of 1979 and women's struggles within the *shoras* expressed how women, in their varied ways, initially experienced the revolution as a liberation. The Islamic state suppressed the secular women's movement, only favouring religious women's organisations and actions. This drove a wedge between these two groups in the 1980s. Secular women's opposition (both inside and outside Iran) to state patriarchy continued and kept women's issues alive and kicking. Religious women resisted the differential treatment meted out to them by the state they gave their support to. As a result, in the 1990s a form of unity had been reached between these groups, despite their social differentiation. Women's participation in economic and political activities had increased gender consciousness, especially among the new generation, who had not experienced the secular way of life experienced by their parents. They constantly put pressure on the state's patriarchal relations. This has produced dynamism within the society as the material and ideological basis of the Islamic state had been brought into question.

Besides organised struggles, women also responded to the patriarchal control of men and the state on an individual basis by choosing different strategies to negotiate with different forms of patriarchy. I have argued that the availability of resources or lack of them, both ideological and material, provided different bases from which women struggled to survive, to secure a better future or improve their status. More importantly, women's organised and individual responses were complementary. Together they generated gender consciousness and, within the Islamic framework, transformed gender relations.

Notes

1. Ettehade Melli Zanan was the biggest women's organisation, affiliated to the Fedayeen.

2. Behdad (1995) argues that in this period the relative income share of poor and middle-income households, in the urban and the rural economy, increased significantly. Clearly the wealthy lost and the poor and the middle class gained from the Islamic state's redistributionist incomes policies.

3. Anas, Atropat Ketab, Ebtekar, Amir Bahador, Badie, Nashre Tarikh, Booteh, Vaystar, Shirazeh, Gil, Asal, Pamchal, Ghesegoo, Mashyaneh, Pirasteh, Rahian Andisheh, Roshangaran Va Motaleateh Zannan, Olume Daneshgahi, Neshaneh, Noavaran, Yasaman, Karang, Tooseheh, Nika, Kayvan, Mafahim, Karnameh, Fereshtegan, Vida, Manouchehri, Gol Aftab, Samir, Hamida, Behtab, Dashtestan, Ghavanin, Kanoon, Hezar Aftab, Shahid Mohebi, Kargaheh Koodak, Nashre Honare Iran, Rahian Sabz, Najin, Sanam, Alhourah, Rafaat, Banoo.

4. Daftare Mosharek Zanan Reyasate Jomhori, Anjomane Hambastegi Zanan, Shabakeh Ertebati Sazemanhayeh Ghayre Dolati Zanan, Mojtamee Najm, Jamiyate Zanan Mohite Zist.

5. *Payame Hajar, Zan, Zanan, Kokab, Mahtab, Hoghoghe Zanan, Zane Rouz.*

6. Najizadeh 1998/9.

7. Marva Nabili and Shahla Riahi.

8. Tahmineh Ardekani, Zahra Mahasti Badiee, Feryal Behzad, Rakhshaneh Bani-Etemadi, Marzieh Borumand, Puran Derakhshandeh, Yasamin Malek Nasr, Samira Makhmalbaf, Tahmineh Milani, Kobra Saeedi.

9. *Banoye Ordibehesht,* the May Lady (1997) by Rakshaneh Bani Etemad, and *Sib,* Apple (1998) by Samira Makhmalbaf.

10. *Bighara* (Turbulent) by Shirin Neshat, 1998; *Talagh* (Divorce, Iranian Style) by Ziba Mir-Hosseini (Iran) and Kim Longinotto (Britain), 1998.

11. Farzaneh, Hoghoghehe Zan, Kokab, Mahtab, Neda, Payame Hajar, Payame Zan, Rouznameh Zan, Zanan, Zane Rouz.

12. Nayereh Akhavan Betaraf, Shahrbano Amani Anganeh, Zahra Pishgahi Fard, Sohaila Jelodarzadeh, Marzieh Jadidchi Dabaghi, Elaheh Rastgo, Fatemeh Ramezanzadeh, Ghodsieh Saiedi Alavi, Marzieh Sadighi, Nafiseh Fayazbakhsh, Monireh Nobakht, Marzieh Vahiddastgherdi, Faezeh Hashemi.

Chapter 7

Conclusion

This book is a contribution to women's resistance to a hostile milieu and their varied struggle for liberation. By analysing changes in women's employment in Islamic Iran, I was able to consider the different sources of oppression that limit women's possibilities in the process of socio-economic and socio-political change. Women experience simultaneously many forms of oppression and engage in a multitude of struggles. These experiences and different struggles for liberation are sometimes contradictory and at other times are harmonious. A significant area of enquiry is the debate between the secular and Muslim feminists on the role of Islamic ideology. I have argued that this debate offers an insight into the oppressive nature of gender roles and relations in Iran. More importantly, the very engagement in this debate tends to bring together the two opposing groups of feminists, both inside and outside Iran.

But the debate is limited in two ways. It is focused mainly on the interrogation of religious ideology, based on textual analysis, and therefore lacks social investigation. More importantly, analysis of gender and economic life is missing from these studies. I hope, therefore, that this analysis of women's employment, grounded in women's material circumstances, will fill this gap. As I have argued throughout the book, in different phases of Islamisation women's employment was determined by the interaction between economic and ideological forces and most importantly by women's various responses to these forces.

The Islamic state, under pressure from socio-economic factors and women's struggles for change, was unable to abolish women's labour. Women's employment in this period did not fall in comparison with the pre-1979 period, even though the Islamic state strengthened patriarchal relationships, which are detrimental to women's employment status. Women's participation in the labour force and the labour market politicised many women, who, through their own experiences, identified a common ground to struggle against a set of oppressive measures by learning to see and know from a different perspective. This approach has enabled them to challenge Islamic theology and thereby the Islamic state.

This analysis enabled me to consider the relationships between capital, state, patriarchy and class system in Iran. I have argued that their operations have been antagonistic as well as collaborative. The role of the state, as affecting and being affected by economic circumstances and ideological factors, has been crucial.

An analysis of the sexual division of labour in the Islamic state demonstrates that the exclusion of women from the labour market adversely affects their standard of living, their contribution to the upward mobility of their families, and their ability to struggle against patriarchal gender relations within the family and the wider society.

This analysis also provides a ground to investigate women's employment within the context of the impact of economic factors and the role of the state in Iran. During the 1980s and 1990s, the Islamic state, as the main agent of economic development and social control, under pressure from economic circumstances, largely adapted to the world economy. Material factors arising from the economic circumstances of the war years had a powerful impact on Islamic ideological attitudes to female participation in the workforce. The process of segregation, which had aimed at the exclusion of women from employment, paradoxically opened up opportunities for many religious women to enter employment. More importantly, women's employment led to contradictions between the theory and the practice of Islamic gender ideology based on *Sharia*. The state had to accommodate to the economic necessity of women's employment. Thus, under economic pressure, state action, even backed by a powerful ideological hegemony, was frustrated in its ability to implement its gender policy.

The main contribution of the empirical work to the debate on gender and employment, however, is the insight that economic policy alone does not determine the inclusion or exclusion of women. The role of the state and its gender ideology is also significant, but this is dynamic, and changes in response to indigenous and global economic circumstances. The Islamic state, despite its criticisms of the Pahlavi system, has remained the agent of economic development; it has maintained capital while strengthening patriarchal relationships in accordance with its gender ideology.

An analysis of social relations of gender under the Islamic state also allowed me to focus on the relationship between women's employment experiences and gender relations in the home and the wider society. Women are not confined and isolated within the domestic space, but are integrated into the workforce differently from men in terms of wage rates and promotion practices. In the process of economic development, patriarchal gender relations have great impact on women's employment. Nevertheless, patriarchal social relations were dynamic. The Islamic state's determination to base gender roles on a traditional interpretation of *Sharia* failed, and it was forced to be pragmatic. Gendered laws and beliefs were changed in response to change in economic circumstances and women's struggle. More importantly, the interaction between economic and ideological factors led to gender consciousness and women's struggle for change. The indigenous class system, combined with different levels of religious adherence and conflicting interests, determined the different ways women rebelled against the system. This is important because, despite extensive critique, western ahistorical ethnocentric depictions of Muslim societies, in which women in Iran appear as the ultimate manifestation of women's oppression, frequently prevail.

This book has demonstrated that the level of gender consciousness is much greater at the end of the 1990s, under the Islamic state, than it was at the height of socio-economic transformation and westernisation in the 1960s and 1970s. The subordination of women in Iran cannot be attributed solely to Islamic ideology and practice. It has to be analysed within a wider perspective, which involves material circumstances and change in gender relations. The overlap or unity between secular and religious women has produced reforms. These reforms are limited, made within the patriarchal Islamic framework where the state is strongly committed to women's subordination to men within the family and the society. The Islamic state, despite its dynamic nature, is a system which severely limits secular women's struggle for a better society, free from religion, and it will hold on to its patriarchal gender relations, as its survival depends on it. Thus, there is still a long way to go. This is an important area of future research and investigation. As long as women continue to struggle, the deeply rooted patriarchal nature of the Islamic state cannot be secured. The women's movement can play a key part in changes which may encompass the entire society.

Appendix

Research in Iran

In summer 1989 I made my first exploratory field work trip to Tehran. My intention was to interview female industrial workers and investigate their employment status before and after the 1979 revolution. I faced enormous problems in the course of gathering evidence. The war with Iraq had ended and Khomeini was dead. Politically there was an atmosphere of chaos and fear everywhere. The majority of the people were suffering as a result of the economic and political crisis. Many who opposed the Islamisation of the state had been executed, disappeared or were still imprisoned. Many, especially those who supported the Islamisation of the state, were either killed in the war with Iraq or were still prisoners of the war, and their families were waiting for their return. Many of these families were left with mentally or physically disabled soldiers who had been sent back home during the war years.

With the help of a woman friend with whom I had been involved in the women's movement in Iran in 1979–81, I interviewed two women from the pharmaceuticals industry and two from the food industry. During 1979–80 we had supported these women outside their factory gates, locked out for struggling to build workers' *shoras* (councils). We helped these women and their colleagues to produce and distribute bulletins. By September 1981 Islamic *shoras* were consolidated in the factories and any independent *shoras* liquidated (Bayat 1987: 100–142; Poya 1987: 143–9). It was no longer possible to participate in these forms of political struggle (see Chapter 6). I returned to London in 1982. My friend worked as a scientist in one of the pharmaceutical firms and continued her contact with some of the women workers, including the four that I interviewed in 1989. Without her it would have been impossible for me to gain access to these women. During the revolution, until 1981, class barriers collapsed between those engaged in political struggle. But they became an obstacle once the political struggles were crushed. Therefore, as far as these women were concerned, I was an outsider, especially since I lived abroad. But they trusted me because of my friend: she worked with them and she came from a religious family, so they could relate to her. Hence they were willing to talk to me.

This was an informal group interview that took place at my friend's house. I used an approach based on the oral history method described by Thompson (1988). I had no pre-set questions, but rather a mental list of all the areas I wanted to cover in the interview. Throughout the interviews I kept the flow to as near to an ordinary conversation as possible. I told the women about myself, my age, my marital status, how many children I had, my occupation, my book and the purpose of my interviews. I then said to them that for objective purposes I also needed some personal details, such as age, marital status, number of children, education and their job.

The data collected from these interviews concerned women's struggle in the workplace during the revolution and after; their conditions of work, their domestic responsibilities, their other forms of work to increase the family income; their relationship to their husbands and other members of their families; and their status within the workplace, the family and society as a whole. These interviews helped me to clarify the research questions.

I returned to Iran in summer 1990 to continue the field research. I lost contact with the four women that I interviewed the previous year. My friend had left her job and she no longer had any 'legitimate' reason to contact those women. The class differences between them could have turned the attention of the authorities to her and to them. Such contact could have been interpreted as being politically motivated against the Islamic state. I had no way of gaining access and so I abandoned concentrating on interviewing industrial workers alone and decided to interview women from different occupations, especially women working for the growing service sector, both in state-owned and privately owned enterprises, as I had more access to this group through my family, my extended family and friends.

In this field trip I interviewed ten women. Some were working in state-owned enterprises as teachers, nurses and bank clerks, others in middle- to small-scale private enterprises as clerks, secretaries or administrative workers. The interviews took place in an atmosphere of fear. The majority of these women, or members of their families, had experienced political persecution by both regimes, of Moham-mad Reza Pahlavi and of Khomeini, and had suffered from the eight-year war with Iraq, economically, politically, socially and personally. They did not feel comfortable talking about their circumstances. Although I explained fully my intention and the purpose of my research as purely an academic exercise, there were still uncertain-ties. I began by asking them general questions about their work history and the relationship between their paid jobs outside the home and their domestic responsibilities. After a few minutes, con-versations became more relaxed and the women felt a common bond, and gradually began to talk to me and answer my questions more willingly.

These interviews allowed me to explore a number of issues in relation to gender, ideology and employment in Iran. For example, what occupations women are concentrated in and why; why, under ideological pressure, women preferred to work in large state-owned enterprises; how women are discriminated against by the labour law as a result of Islamic gender ideology; how women lose benefits, pensions and years of service; how women's exclusive responsibility for the reproduction and maintenance of the family place them in a disadvantaged position within the home and at paid work outside the home; and how, in the majority of cases, husbands and male members of the family, under the influence of gender ideology, disapprove of women working outside the home. But in cases where a family needed the woman's financial contribution, the man had no choice other than to permit her to go out to work. We discussed how the policy and practice of segregation imposed by the Islamic state opened up opportunities for many women to enter employ-ment. Even those women who opposed compulsory Islamic dress agreed with those who supported this policy that segregation had created space for women. Finally we explored how women mobilise ideological and material resources to cope with the conflicts arising from their participation in the labour market.

Each interview added something to my knowledge. I found women's personal and work histories empowering, validating the importance of their experience. Gluck and Patai (1991: 2) argue that for this reason oral history work with women is assumed to be inherently feminist. My purpose in interviewing women was not just to seek information or evidence of value in itself. It was, on the one hand, to make a subjective record of how each woman looked back at her life and work history, what she emphasised, what she missed out, the words she used to express a particular feeling (Thompson 1988: 196–205), and, on the other hand, how women struggle in and outside the home in order to improve the standard of living of their families and their own status in relation to men.

At this stage I decided to use structured questionnaires to obtain comparative evidence, using the interviews to raise questions and the questionnaires to gauge the validity of some of the answers in the interviews. The questionnaires were also designed as a comparative measure, alongside the interviews, to analyse women's place in the workforce, their employment status, level of education, fertility rate, class and level of religious observance, the degree of decision-making within the family and the effect of their domestic responsibilities on their paid work and vice versa. The aim was to examine the degree of awareness, struggle and change for women of different social groups. With the help of my daughters, my sister and women of my extended family, we produced five hundred questionnaires. These questionnaires went from hand to hand to women in schools, nursery schools, universities, factories, offices, hospitals and banks, and to the homes of women engaged in self-employment and voluntary work.

In summer 1991 I made another trip to Iran and interviewed fifty-six women. In Tehran, I visited schools, banks, hospitals, medium-sized private enterprises, industrial firms and newspapers. These visits were made possible by friends and relatives who obtained permission through the authorities. All workplaces and individual women agreed to distribute and collect my questionnaires.

In some workplaces men and women were segregated into different spaces – rooms or assembly lines – but in others they worked together. In some workplaces, male and female workers' lunch breaks and prayer times were at different times: for example women's lunch break was 12.30–1.00 p.m. and prayer 1.00–1.30; men's lunch 1.00–1.30 and prayer 1.30–2.00. In other workplaces there was no official segregation, but usually women ate together and prayed together.

Some of these interviews took place at work; they were formal, and opportunities to talk freely were very limited, as officials were present. Others took place in the homes of the interviewees, were informal and more relaxed. I used different styles: a friendly, informal, conversational approach with women who I knew quite well and was interviewing at home; a more formal, controlled style of questioning with women who I did not know and interviewed at work. Finch (1984) and Oakley (1981) argue that less structured research strategies, which avoid creating a hierarchical relationship between interviewer and interviewee, are more suitable than formal, survey-type interviewing because informal interviews do not turn women into objects. They also criticise the view that the interviewer should remain detached, distant and in control. However, for the purpose of my research a combination of both formal and informal interviews proved to be necessary.

I also travelled to a number of villages in Khorasan province, in eastern Iran. This area is one of the biggest centres of carpet-weaving and agricultural production. It is very poor in terms of climate and resources; water is extremely scarce as the area is close to the desert; people's standard of living is poor and the level of education and health is very low. In these villages, men and women worked on the land throughout the year producing grapes, pistachio nuts, cumin, saffron, cotton, wheat and barley. Women were also carpet-weavers. Men were the heads of households; they dealt with officials, middlemen, and the buying and selling of materials. Women hardly went out of the village. The carpet-weaving was mainly the job of women and young girls, taking place in the houses. In each house the room for carpet-weaving is also the sitting room. These rooms are called *kargahe khanegi* (household workshop). Men are the *karfarma* (employer) and women are *ghalibaf* (carpet-weavers). These villages were self-sufficient: there were no shops; women produced all the family's clothes and daily food (bread, butter, cheese, vegetables and fruit). Women also performed animal husbandry, mainly for the men to sell the animals or their produce in the market. To compare the condition of women carpet-weavers and agricultural workers of this area to those of a richer area, I also travelled to a number of villages in Mazandaran, in the north of Iran, where the climate is good, resources not so scarce and people have a better standard of living and a higher level of health and of education. In this area women were engaged in the production of rice and tea, as well as in carpet-weaving.

In these interviews I learned about women's tasks, the difference between their jobs and men's jobs; how important their contribution is to their family; what they do when they go home; what housework is carried out by men (if any); what it means for women to work; and whether it means more autonomy in decision-making about themselves, their children and family expenditure. These issues emerged from the previous year's interviews. This time I used these questions explicitly while at the same time allowing new points to be developed out of each conversation. This restructuring of the questions was very fruitful as it allowed me to compare different women's experiences and strategies.

I thought about the sequence of topics and let questions lead naturally from one to another. These questions allowed a more detailed understanding of the sexual division of labour and the benefits of women's work to their families. Women of all classes and levels of religious faith are exclusively responsible for domestic work. The neglect of this responsibility is socially and culturally unacceptable within the family and the society. As I discuss in Chapter 5, women could work an average of 14–15 hours per day. I was also able to understand the social relations between men and women and the ways in which women of different class and religious profiles chose material and ideological resources to cope with gender ideology, and, most importantly, how they struggled to improve their status at home, at work and in the wider society.

The oral history method of using the detailed memories of the interviewees (Thompson 1988: 201) proved fruitful. Women's work histories had a dimension of female struggle against a hostile environment (Borland 1991: 67). Although only a few would identify themselves with feminism and feminist ideas, the questions that I asked encouraged women to think about their status (Gluck and

Patai 1991: 205) and the discrimination against them. They welcomed my intention to raise the question of how important women's work is to their families and to the Iranian economy and society. On this trip I collected 200 questionnaires. I did not know many of the women who helped me to distribute them. They agreed to do so as friends or family.

In 1992 I interviewed ten women who were buying cheaply and selling expensively in the black market. There are a large number of women engaged in this work. This was a group interview in Tehran in the home of one of them. She asked nine other women in her neighbourhood to join her and tell their stories as petty commodity producers and sellers. I asked them the same questions raised in the previous interviews. I learned that their earnings and their contribution are indispensable to their families. As discussed in Chapter 4, they do not count in the statistics, although without their contribution their families would not survive the inflation and male unemployment.

This time, I collected 148 questionnaires. These together with those collected in 1991 comprised: 31 voluntary workers, 35 self-employed, 50 industrial workers, 40 VDU operators, 28 nurses, 53 teachers, 55 administrative workers and clerks, and 56 technicians, engineers, scientists and librarians.

When I started my interviews, I did not know, because of political constraints, how many women, in what occupations, I would have access to. So I took my chances wherever possible. But this wide range of interviews with women across different occupations, different classes and different degrees of religious observance proved useful.

Open-ended and semi-structured interviews are time-consuming, but each had its own characteristic features and provided useful information which fitted into the general picture. There was a snowball effect as they conveyed women's experiences and views, which led to new ideas and dimensions. The semi-structured interviews provided some scope for interviewees' interpretations, but it also allowed compararison with others. Interviewing women from different occupations and religious backgrounds minimised bias, because they represent different types of experience in relation to women and employment in Iran.

Statistical analysis of my structured questionnaires furnished considerable standardised factual information, which allowed comparison and generalisation. However, I am aware that at workplaces the questionnaires had to go through security systems, and people were generally more nervous of putting their words into writing than of saying them in conversation. Some completed the questionnaires fully and made comments. Others did not fully complete them. Also the preset questions in the questionnaires could be misunderstood. For this reason, I tested the reliability of the answers by comparing them with the answers given to the same question in the interviews.

I also studied volumes of official statistics from the Ministry of Labour, the Plan and Budgets Organisation and the national statistical centre. From this I extracted statistics in relation to women's employment, education and fertility. My aim was to analyse to what extent this information supported the answers given in the interviews. In addition, I produced statistics from my questionnaires and interviews in relation to women's fertility rate, education, employment status, hours of work and level of earnings and compared them with official (men's) indicators of women's status to see to what extent access to paid employment or the lack of it affect their autonomy and degree of decision-making.

The statistical data is from different periods. In Chapters 2 and 3 I have used statistics published by the Pahlavi regime in 1978. In Chapters 4 and 5 I have used statistics published by the Islamic state in the 1980s and 1990s. Statistics based on gender distribution are not available in systematic form from either the Pahlavi or the Islamic regime. I have therefore used those statistics available for the state sector and the private sector of the economy in the selected years that show gender distribution.

Furthermore I use daily newspapers and women's magazines published under the Pahlavi, under the Islamic state and by the opposition to each, both in Farsi and in English. The data collected from this source addressed changes in women's education, employment and fertility rate; Islamic laws and regulations concerning women and the family; and women's reaction and attitude to these changes. In the first eighteen months after the 1979 revolution the media were independent of the state. Once the state consolidated its power the media were totally controlled. However, as is discussed in Chapter 6, in the 1990s a form of pluralism came into existence within the Islamic framework. Some of the media express this pluralism. Different socio-economic and socio-political issues are published and produced – with the exception of blasphemous issues, which are not tolerated and are subject to severe punishment.

Study of the constitutions (1909 and 1980) and the labour laws of the Pahlavi and the Islamic state, together with other research in Farsi and in English, were also essential. This enabled me to collect information about women's position generally and specifically in relation to employment in different periods and from different points of view. As I discuss in Chapter 2, the similarities and differences between the Pahlavi state and the Islamic state made me aware of the problem of continuity and change in relation to gender and employment.

I carried out the field research between 1989 and 1992 and since then I have visited Iran regularly. In these visits I have observed changes in the socio-economic and socio-political situation and the effect of these changes on women, in particular in relation to women and employment. I have also visited some of my interviewees and observed the change in their attitudes to Islamic dress, their domestic work, their paid work outside the home, their standard of living, working conditions and men's attitude to women's contribution to the well-being of the family. I have also observed an increasing interest in women's issues throughout society expressed in the media, especially through television and radio, which are widely used even in villages. I observed women's and men's attitude to changes in relation to women's issues, such as the role of women in the 1996 parliamentary election and changes in legislation in relation to women and work.

Bibliography

Abrahamian, E. (1982) *Iran Between Two Revolutions*, Princeton University Press, Princeton NJ.

Acker, J. (1973) 'Women and Social Stratification: A Case of Intellectual Sexism', in *American Journal of Sociology*, vol. 78, no. 4.

Adamiyat, F. and H. Nategh (1978) *Afkare ejtemaiy siasi va eghtesadi dar asare montasher nashodehe dowrane Qajar* (The Social, Political and Economic Thought of the Qajar Period in unpublished documents), Kharazmi Publication, Iran.

Afkhami, M. and E. Friedl (1994) *Women in Post-revolutionary Iran*, I.B. Tauris, London and New York.

Afshar, H. (1982) 'Khomeini's Teachings and Their Implications for Iranian Women', in A. Tabari and N. Yeganeh, eds., *In the Shadow of Islam: The Women's Movement in Iran*, Zed Books, London.

Afshar, H. (1985) 'The Position of Women in an Iranian Village', in H. Afshar, ed., *Women, Work and Ideology in the Third World*, Tavistock, London.

Afshar, H. (1987) 'Women, Marriage and the State in Iran', in H. Afshar, ed., *Women, State and Ideology*, Macmillan, London.

Afshar, H. (1989) 'Women and Work: Ideology Not Adjustment at Work in Iran', in H. Afshar, ed., *Women, Poverty and Ideology in Asia*, Macmillan, London.

Afshar, H. (1991) 'The Emancipation Struggles in Iran: Past Experiences and Future Hopes', in H. Afshar, ed., *Women, Development and Survival in the Third World*, Longman, London and New York.

Afshar, H. (1994) 'Women and the Politics of Fundamentalism in Iran', *Women Against Fundamentalism Journal*, no. 5, London.

Afshar, H. (1998) *Islam and Feminisms: An Iranian Case-Study*, Macmillan, London.

Agarwal, B. (1988) *Structures of Patriarchy: State, Community and Household in Modernising Asia*, Zed Books, London.

Algar, H. (1969) *Religion and State in Iran 1785–1906*, University of California Press, Berkeley, Los Angeles and London.

Algar, H. (1980) *The Constitution of the Islamic Republic of Iran*, Mizan Press, Berkeley.

Algar, H. (1981) *Islamic Government, in Writing and Declarations of Imam Khomeini*, Mizan Press, Berkeley.

Al-Hibri, A. (1981) 'Capitalism is an Advanced Stage of Patriarchy: but Marxism is Not Feminism', in L. Sargent, ed., *Women and Revolution: A Discussion of the Unhappy Marriage of Marxism and Feminism*, South End Press, Boston MA.

Anderson, K. and D.C. Jack (1991) 'Learning to Listen, Interview Techniques and Analyses', in S.B. Gluck and D. Patai, eds., *Women's Words: The Feminist Practice of Oral History*, Routledge, London and New York.

Azad, A. (1987/8 – date of translation) *Zanane Irani va Raho Rasme Zendegie Anan, Safarnameh Clara Rice* (Persian Women and Their Ways by Clara Colliver Rice), Ghodse Razavi Publication, Iran.

Azari, F. (1983) *Women of Iran: The Conflict with Fundamentalist Islam*, Ithaca Press, London.

Bahar, S. (1983) 'A Historical Background to the Women's Movement in Iran', in F. Azari, ed., *Women of Iran: The Conflict with Fundamentalist Islam*, Ithaca Press, London.

Bakhash, S.H. (1978) *Iran: Monarchy, Bureaucracy and Reform under the Qajars: 1858–1896*, Ithaca Press, London.

Bakhash, S.H. (1985) *The Reign of the Ayatollahs, Iran and the Islamic Revolution*, I.B. Tauris, London.

Barrett, M. (1988) *Women's Oppression Today: The Marxist/Feminist Encounter*, Verso, London and New York.

Bartsch, W.H. (1977) 'The Industrial Labour Force of Iran: Problems of Recruitment, Training and Productivity', in J.A. Momeni, ed., *The Population of Iran, A Selection of Readings*, East West Population Institute, Pahlavi University, USA.

Bauman, Z. (1982) *Memories of Class*, Routledge & Kegan Paul, London.

Bayat, A. (1987) *Workers and Revolution in Iran*, Zed Books, London and New Jersey.

Bayat-Philipp, M. (1978) 'Women and Revolution in Iran, 1905–1911', in L. Beck and N. Keddie, eds., *Women in the Muslim World*, Harvard University Press, Cambridge MA and London.

Beck, L. (1978) 'Women among Qashqai Nomadic Pastoralists in Iran', in L. Beck and N. Keddie, eds., *Women in the Muslim World*, Harvard University Press, Cambridge MA and London.

Behdad, S. (1995a) 'The Post-Revolutionary Economic Crisis', in S. Rahnema and S. Behdad, eds., *Iran After the Revolution*, I.B. Tauris, London and New York.

Behdad, S. (1995b) 'From Economic Populism to Economic Liberalism in Iran: There Ain't No Miracles No More', paper presented at the Controversies On Revolution And Development In Iran conference, Guildhall University of London, 10 June 1995.

Behnam, J. (1977) 'Population', in J.A. Momeni, ed., *The Population of Iran: A*

Selection of Readings, East West Population Institute, Pahlavi University, USA.

Beneria, L. and M. Roldan (1987) *The Crossroads of Class and Gender: Industrial Homework, Subcontracting and Household Dynamics in Mexico City*, University of Chicago Press, Chicago and London.

Beneria, L. and G. Sen (1981) 'Accumulation, Reproduction and Women's Role in Economic Development: Boserup Revisited', in *Signs: Journal of Women in Culture and Society*, USA.

Bernstein, H. (1994) 'Agrarian Classes in Capitalist Development', in L. Sklair, ed., *Capitalism and Development*, Routledge, London and New York.

Bernstein, H., H. Johnson and A. Thomas (1992) 'Labour Regimes and Social Change under Colonialism', in T. Allen and A. Thomas, eds., *Poverty and Development in the 1990s*, Oxford University Press, Oxford.

Bharier, J. (1977) 'A Note on the Population of Iran, 1900–1966', in J.A. Momeni, ed., *The Population of Iran: A Selection of Readings*, East West Population Institute, Pahlavi University, USA.

Borland, K. (1991) '"That's Not What I Said": Interpretive Conflict in Oral Narrative Research', in S.B. Gluck and D. Patai, eds., *Women's Words: The Feminist Practice of Oral History*, Routledge, New York and London.

Bornet, J. (1992) 'Collecting and Analysing Oral Evidence', in M. Drake, R. Finnegan and J. Eustace, eds., *Studying Family and Community History, 19th and 20th Centuries, Volume 4, Sources and Methods: A Handbook*, Open University Press, Milton Keynes.

Boserup, E. (1987) *Women's Role in Economic Development*, Gower, Aldershot.

Braverman, H. (1974) *Labour and Monopoly Capital*, Monthly Review Press, New York.

Browne, E.G. (1910) *The Persian Revolution of 1905–1909*, Cambridge University Press, Cambridge.

Callinicos, A. (1983) 'The New Middle Class and Socialist Politics', *International Socialism Journal*, vol. 2, no. 20, London.

Chanfrault-Duchet, M.F. (1991) 'Narrative Structures, Social Models and Symbolic Representation in the Life Story', in S.B. Gluck and D. Patai, eds., *Women's Words: The Feminist Practice of Oral History*, Routledge, New York and London.

Chhachhi, A. (1991) 'Forced Identities: The State, Communalism, Fundamentalism and Women in India', in D. Kandiyoti, ed., *Women, Islam and the State*, Macmillan, London.

Cohen, G.A. (1978) *Karl Marx's Theory of History*, Princeton University Press, Princeton NJ.

Coulson, M., B. Magaš and H. Wainwright (1975) 'The Housewife and Her Labour under Capitalism: A Critique', *New Left Review* no. 89.

Crow, B., M. Thorpe *et al.* (1988) *Survival and Change in the Third World*, Polity Press, Cambridge.

Degras, J. (1950) *The Communist International* Vol. 1, Oxford University Press, London.

De Groot, J. (1996) 'Gender, Discourse and Ideology in Iranian Studies: Towards a New Scholarship', in D. Kandiyoti, ed., *Gendering the Middle East,*

Emerging Perspectives, I.B. Tauris, London.

Elson, D. and R. Pearson (1984) 'The Subordination of Women and the Internationalisation of Factory Production', in K. Young, C. Wolkowitz and R. McCullagh, eds., *Of Marriage and the Market:Women's Subordination Internationally and its Lessons*, Routledge, London.

Etezadi Tabatabai, S. (1979) in *Islamic Revolution*, July.

Etezadi Tabatabai, S. (1981) in *Zane Rouz*, June.

Fallaci, O. (1976) *Interview with History*, Houghton Mifflin, Boston.

Farhadpour, L. (1998) in *Gosaresh*, January.

Finch, J. (1984) '"It's Great to Have Someone to Talk To": The Ethics and Politics of Interviewing Women', in C. Bell and H. Roberts, eds., *Social Researching, Politics, Problems, Practice*, Routledge and Kegan Paul, London.

Finnegan, R. (1992) 'Studying Family and Community History', in M. Drake, R. Finnegan and J. Eustace, eds., *Studying Family and Community History, 19th and 20th Centuries, Volume 4, Sources and Methods: A Handbook*, Open University Press, Milton Keynes.

Fischer, M.J. (1978) 'On Changing the Concept and Position of Persian Women', in L. Beck and N. Keddie, eds., *Women in the Muslim World*, Harvard University Press, Cambridge MA and London.

Gardiner, J. (1977) 'Women in the Labour Process and Class Structure', in Alan Hunt, ed., *Class and Class Structure*, Lawrence & Wishart, London.

Gluck, S.B. and D. Patai, eds. (1991) *Women's Words: The Feminist Practice of Oral History*, Routledge, New York and London.

Goetz, A.M. (1991) 'Feminism and the Claim to Know: Contradictions in Feminist Approaches to Women and Development', in R. Grant and K. Newland, eds., *Gender and International Relations*, Open University Press, Milton Keynes.

Gorz, A. (1982) *Goodbye to the Working Class*, Pluto Press, London.

Graham, H. (1983) 'Do Her Answers Fit His Questions? Women and the Survey Method', in E. Gamarnikow, D. Morgan, J. Purvis and D. Taylorson, eds., *The Public and the Private*, Heinemann, London.

Grown, C.A. and J. Sebstad (1989) 'Introduction: Toward a Wider Perspective on Women's Employment', *World Development*, vol. 17, no. 7, Pergamon Press, Oxford.

Haeri, S. (1989) *Law of Desire: Temporary Marriage in Iran*, I.B. Tauris, London and New York.

Haeri, S. (1994) 'Temporary Marriage: An Islamic Discourse on Female Sexuality in Iran', in M. Afkhami and E. Friedl, *Women in Post-revolutionary Iran*, I.B. Tauris, London and New York.

Haggis, J. (1990) 'The Feminist Research Process – Defining a Topic', in L. Stanley, ed, *Feminist Praxis*, Routledge, London and New York.

Halliday, F. (1979) *Iran: Dictatorship and Development*, Penguin, London and New York.

Harding, S. (1987) 'Is there a Feminist Method?', in S. Harding, ed., *Feminism and Methodology*, Open University Press, Milton Keynes.

Hashemi, F. (1980) in *Ettellaat*, 28 July.

Hashemi, F. (1981) in *Zane Rouz*, June.

Hendessi, M. (1990) 'Armed Angels: Women in Iran', *Change Report*, no. 16, London.

Hendessi, M. and Shafii, R. (1995) 'Women and Politics of Fundamentalism in Iran', *Women Against Fundamentalism Journal*.

Higgins, P.J. and P. Shoar-Ghaffari (1994) 'Women's Education in the Islamic Republic of Iran', in M. Afkhami and E. Friedl, eds., *Women in Post-revolutionary Iran*, I.B. Tauris, London and New York.

Hobsbawm, E. (1981) 'The Forward March of Labour Halted?' and 'Observations on the Debate', in M. Jacques and F. Mulhern, eds., *The Forward March of Labour Halted?*, New Left Books, London.

Humphrey, J. (1987) *Gender and Work in the Third World, Sexual Divisions in Brazilian Industry*, Tavistock, London.

Issawi, C. (1971) *The Economic History of Iran*, University of Chicago Press, Chicago and London.

Jayaratne, T.E. (1983) 'The Value of Quantitative Methodology for Feminist Research', in Bowles and R. Duelli Klein, eds., *Theories of Women's Studies*, Routledge & Kegan Paul, London.

Jayaratne, T.E. and A.J. Stewart (1991) 'Quantitative and Qualitative Methods in the Social Sciences, Current Feminist Issues and Practical Strategies', in M.M. Fonow and J.A. Cook, eds., *Beyond Methodology, Feminist Scholarship as Lived Research*, Indiana University Press, Bloomington.

Jayawardena, K. (1986) *Feminism and Nationalism in the Third World*, Zed Books, London.

Kaar, M. (1997) 'The Situation of Women in Iran: Round Table', paper presented at the Re-Thinking Islam: Politics British Society for Middle Eastern Society conference, St Catherine's College, University of Oxford.

Kabeer, N. (1994) *Revised Realities*, Verso, London.

Kandiyoti, D. (1991) 'Islam and Patriarchy: A Comparative Perspective', in N. Keddie and B. Brown, eds., *Women in Middle-Eastern History*, Yale University Press, New Haven and London.

Kandiyoti, D. (1996) 'Contemporary Feminist Scholarship and Middle East Studies', in D. Kandiyoti, ed., *Gendering the Middle-East: Emerging Perspectives*, I.B. Tauris, London and New York.

Kay, G. (1979) *The Economic Theory of the Working Class*, Macmillan, London.

Kazemi, F. (1980) *Poverty and Revolution in Iran*, New York University.

Keddie, N.R. (1966) *Religion and Rebellion in Iran: The Tobacco Protest of 1891–1892*, Frank Cass, London.

Keddie, N.R. (1981) *Roots of Revolution: An Interpretive History of Modern Iran*, Yale University Press, New Haven and London.

Khomeini, R. (1979) *Towzih almasael* (Explanation of Problems), Tehran Pirouz, Iran.

Khomeini, R. (1366; 1987/8) *Symayeh Zan Dar Kalameh Imam Khomeini* (Women in Imam Khomeini's Words), Vezarate Farhang va Ershade Eslami (The Ministry of Culture and Islamic Guidance), Iran.

Kian, A. (1997) 'Women and Politics in Post-Islamist Iran: The Gender

Conscious Drive to Change', British Journal of Middle Eastern Studies, vol. 24, no. 1, London.

Lukes, S. (1984) 'The Future of British socialism?', in B. Pimlott, ed., Fabian Essays in Socialist Thought, Heinemann, London.

Mackintosh, M. (1984) 'Gender and Economics: The Sexual Division of Labour and the Subordination of women', in K. Young, C. Wolkowitz and R. McCullagh, eds., Of Marriage and the Market: Women's Subordination Internationally and its Lessons, Routledge, London.

Mackintosh, M. (1989) Gender, Class and Rural Transition: Agrobusiness and the Food Crisis in Senegal, Zed Books, London.

Majlesi, M.B. (1979) Hilyat olmuttaqin (The Ornament of the Pious), Qaem, Iran.

Mandel, E. (1978) 'Introduction', in K. Marx, Capital Vol. 2, Penguin Books, Harmondsworth.

Marx, K. (1956) Capital Vol. 2, Progress Publishers, Moscow.

Marx, K. (1980) Capital Vol. 1, Penguin Books, Harmondsworth.

Matini, J. (1989) 'The Impact of the Islamic Revolution on Education in Iran', in A. Badran, ed., At the Crossroads: Education in the Middle East, Paragon House, New York.

Mehran, G. (1989) 'Socialisation of Schoolchildren in the Islamic Republic of Iran', Iranian Studies, The Journal of the Society of Iranian Studies, vol. 22, no. 1, USA.

Mernissi, F. (1987) Beyond the Veil, Indiana University Press, Bloomington.

Mies, M. (1986) Patriarchy and Accumulation On a World Scale: Women in the International Division of Labour, Zed Books, London and New Jersey.

Mies, M. (1994) 'Gender and Global Capitalism', in L. Sklair, ed., Capitalism and Development, Routledge, London and New York.

Milani, F. (1985) 'Conformity and Confrontation: A Comparison of Two Iranian Women Poets', in E. Warnock Fernea, ed., Women and the Family in the Middle East, New Voices of Change, University of Texas Press, Austin.

Mir-Hosseini, Z. (1993a) Marriage on Trial, A Study of Islamic Family Law: Iran and Morocco Compared, I.B. Tauris, London and New York.

Mir-Hosseini, Z. (1993b) 'Women, Marriage and the Law in Post-Revolutionary Iran', in H. Afshar, ed., Women in the Middle East: Perceptions, Realities and Struggles for Liberation, Macmillan, London.

Mir-Hosseini, Z. (1996) 'Stretching the Limits: A Feminist Reading of the Sharia in Post-Khomeini Iran', in M. Yamani, ed., Feminism and Islam, Ithaca Press, London.

Moaddel, M. (1991) 'Class Structure in Post-Revolutionary Iran', International Journal of Middle East Studies, vol. 23, USA.

Moghadam, F.E. (1994) 'Commoditisation of Sexuality and Female Labour, Participation in Islam: Implications for Iran 1960–1990', in M. Afkhami and E. Friedl, eds., Women in Post-revolutionary Iran, I.B. Tauris, London and New York.

Moghadam, V. (1988) 'Women, Work and Ideology in the Islamic Republic', International Journal of Middle East Studies, vol. 20, no. 2, pp. 221–43, Cambridge University Press, Cambridge.

Moghadam, V. (1993a) 'Women in the Islamic Republic of Iran: Inequality, Accommodation, Resistance', in V. Moghadam, *Modernizing Women, Gender and Social Change in the Middle East*, Lynne Rienner Publishers, Boulder CO.

Moghadam, V. (1993b) 'Women, Patriarchy, and the Changing Family', in V. Moghadam, *Modernizing Women, Gender and Social Change in the Middle East*, Lynne Rienner Publishers, Boulder CO.

Mohsenpour, B. (1988) 'Philosophy of Education in Postrevolutionary Iran', *Comparative Education Review*, vol. 32, no. 1, USA.

Mojab, S. (1987) 'The Islamic Government's Policy on Women's Access to Higher Education and its Impact on the Socio-economic Status of Women', Working Paper no. 156, Michigan State University.

Molyneux, M. (1985) 'Mobilisation without Emancipation? Women's Interests, the State and Revolution in Nicaragua', *Feminist Studies*, no. 11, University of Maryland.

Morgan, D. (1981) 'Men, Masculinity and the Process of Sociological Enquiry', in H. Roberts, ed., *Doing Feminist Research*, Routledge & Kegan Paul, London and New York.

Mottahari, M. (1981) *The Right of Women in Islam*, World Organisation for Islamic Services, Iran.

Nafisi, H. (1994) 'Veiled Vision/Powerful Presences: Women in Postrevolutionary Iranian Cinema', in M. Afkhami and E. Friedl, *Women in Post-revolutionary Iran*, I.B. Tauris, London and New York.

Nahid, A. (1981) *Zanane Iran Dar Jonbeshe Mashroteh* (Iranian Women in the Constitutional Movement), Tehran.

Najizadeh, F. (1998/9) 'Masomiat Farhangi' (Cultural Innocence) in Gofteman, *Our Words*, Vaystar Publications.

Najmabadi, A. (1991) 'Hazards of Modernity and Morality: Women, State and Ideology in Contemporary Iran', in D. Kandiyoti, ed., *Women, Islam and the State*, Macmillan, London.

Nash, J. and M.P. Fernandez Kelly (1985) *Women, Men and the International Division of Labour*, SUNY Press, New York.

Nashat, G. (1983) *Women and Revolution in Iran*, Westview Press, Boulder CO.

Nomani, F. and A. Rahnema (1994) *Islamic Economic Systems*, Zed Books, London and New Jersey.

Nouri, Y. (1343; 1964/5) *Hughughe Zan Dar Iran va Jahan* (Women's Rights in Iran and the World), Tehran.

Oakley, A. (1972) *Sex, Gender and Society*, Temple Smith, London.

Oakley, A. (1981) 'Interviewing Women: A Contradiction in Term', in S. Roberts, ed., *Doing Feminist Research*, Routledge & Kegan Paul, London and New York.

Offe, C. (1985) 'Work: the Key Sociological Category?', in C. Offe, *Disorganised Capitalism*, Polity Press, Cambridge.

Paidar, P. (1996) 'Feminism and Islam in Iran', in D. Kandiyoti, ed., *Gendering the Middle East: Emerging Perspectives*, I.B. Tauris, London and New York.

Paidar, P. (1997) *Women and the Political Process in Twentieth-Century Iran*, Cambridge University Press, Cambridge.

Pakizehgi, B. (1978) 'Legal and Social Positions of Iranian Women', in L. Beck and N. Keddie, eds., *Women in the Muslim World*, Harvard University Press, Cambridge MA and London.

Pearson, R. (1992) 'Gender Issues in Industrialisation', in T. Hewitt, J. Johnson and D. Wield, eds., *Industrialisation and Development*, Oxford University Press, Oxford.

Pearson, R. (1994) 'Gender Relations, Capitalism and Third World Industrialisation', in L. Sklair, ed., *Capitalism and Development*, Routledge, London and New York.

Pesaran, M.H. (1995) 'An Overview of Stabilisation Policies in Iran', paper presented at the Controversies On Revolution And Development In Iran conference, Guildhall University of London, 10 June 1995.

Poulantzas, N. (1975) *Class in Contemporary Capitalism*, New Left Books, London.

Poulantzas, N. (1987) *Political Power and Social Classes*, Verso, London and New York.

Poya, M. (1987) 'IRAN 1979: Long live Revolution! ... Long live Islam?', in C. Barker, ed., *Revolutionary Rehearsals*, Bookmarks, London.

Poya, M. (1991) 'The Role of Iran in the Gulf War', in H. Bresheeth and N. Yuval-Davis, eds., *The Gulf War and the New World Order*, Zed Books, London and New Jersey.

Poya, M. (1992) 'Double Exile, Iranian Women and Fundamentalism', in N. Yuval Davis and G. Sahgal, eds., *Refusing Holy Orders, Women and Fundamentalism in Britain*, Virago, London.

Pugh, A. (1990) 'My Statistics and Feminism – A True Story', in L. Stanley, ed., *Feminist Praxis*, Routledge, London and New York.

Quran (1955) trans. A.J. Arberry, Centre for Islamic Studies, Iran.

Rahman, F. (1983) 'Status of Women in the Quran', in G. Nashat, ed., *Women and Revolution in Iran*, Westview Press, Boulder CO.

Rahnavard, Z. (n.d.) *Toloueh Zane Mosalman* (The Rise of Muslim Woman), Mahboubeh Publications, Iran.

Rahnema, A. (1994) 'Ali Shariati: Teacher, Preacher, Rebel', in A. Rahnema, *Pioneers of Islamic Revival*, Zed Books, London and New Jersey.

Rahnema, A. (1998) *The Islamic Utopian, A Political Biography of Ali Shariati*, I.B. Tauris, London and New York.

Rahnema, A. and F. Nomani (1990) *The Secular Miracle: Religion, Politics and Economic Policy in Iran*, Zed Books, London and New Jersey.

Razaghi, E. (1988/9) *Eghtesade Iran* (Iran's Economy), Nay Publications, Iran.

Rose, G. (1983) 'Velayate Faghih and the Recovery of Islamic Identity in the Thought of Ayatollah Khomeini', in N.R. Keddie, ed., *Religion and Politics in Iran*, Yale University Press, New Haven and London.

Rubin, G. (1975) 'The Traffic in Women', in R. Reiter, ed., *Toward an Anthropology of Women*, Monthly Review Press, New York.

Saffioti, H. (1978) *Women in Class Society*, Monthly Review Press, New York.

Sanasarian, E. (1982) *The Women's Rights Movement in Iran: Mutiny, Appeasement and Repression from 1900 to Khomeini*, Praeger, Washington DC.

Sanasarian, E. (1986) 'Political Activism and Islamic Identity in Iran', in L. Iglitzen and R. Ross, eds., *Women in the World*, ABC-Clif, Santa Barbara CA.

Sargent, L. (1981) *Women and Revolution: A Discussion of the Unhappy Marriage of Marxism and Feminism*, South End Press, Boston MA.

Sen, G. and C. Grown (1987) *Development, Crises and Alternative Visions: Third World Women's Perspectives*, Monthly Review Press, New York.

Seyf, A. (1373; 1994/5) *Eghtesade Iran Dar Gharneh Nouzdahom* (Iran's Economy in the Nineteenth Century), Cheshmeh Publications, Iran.

Shahidi, H. (1997) 'Women in Iranian Journalism 1910–1998', paper presented at the Gender and Society in the Muslim World since 1800 seminar, Royal Holloway College, University of London, 4 July 1997.

Shariati, A. (1990) *Fatimah is Fatimah*, Shariati Foundation, Iran.

Shariati, A. (1369; 1990/1) *Zan, Majmoueh Assar* (Women, Collected Work), Chappakhsh, Iran.

Squires, J.A. (1989) 'The Contribution of Contemporary Feminist Political Theory to the Public/Private Debate', Ph.D thesis, Queen Mary College, University of London.

Stacey, M. (1981) 'The Division of Labour Revisited, or Overcoming the Two Adams', in P. Abrams et al., eds., *Development and Diversity: British Sociology 1950–1980*, Allen & Unwin, London.

Stanley, Liz (1990) 'Feminist Praxis and the Academic Mode of Production', in L. Stanley, ed., *Feminist Praxis*, Routledge, London and New York.

Tabari, A. (1982) 'Islam and the Struggle for Emancipation of Iranian Women', in A. Tabari and N. Yeganeh, *In the Shadow of Islam: The Women's Movement in Iran*, Zed Press, London.

Tabari, A. (1983) 'The Role of the Clergy in Modern Iranian Politics', in N. Keddie, ed., *Religion and Politics in Iran*, Yale University Press, New Haven and London.

Tabari, A. and N. Yeganeh (1982) *In the Shadow of Islam: The Women's Movement in Iran*, Zed Books, London.

Tabatabai, A. (1358; 1979/80) *Zan Dar Eslam* (Women in Islam), Maktabe Tashyah, Qom.

Tinker, I. (1990) *Persistent Inequalities: Women and World Development*, Oxford University Press, New York.

Thompson, P. (1988) *The Voice of the Past*, Oxford University Press, Oxford and New York.

Tohidi, N. (1996) '*Feminisme Eslami*': *Chaleshi Demokratik Ya Charkheshi Teocratic?* ('Islamic feminism': a democratic challenge or theocratic change?), Nashrieh Bonyade Pajoheshhaye Zanan Iran, California.

Walby, S. (1990) *Theorizing Patriarchy*, Blackwell, Oxford and Cambridge MA.

Ward, K. (1990) *Women Workers and Global Restructuring*, Ithaca Press, New York.

Warnock Fernea, E. and B. Qattan Bezirgan (1977) *Middle Eastern Muslim Women Speak*, University of Texas Press, Austin and London.

Whitehead, A. (1979) 'Some Preliminary Notes on the Subordination of Women', *IDS Bulletin*, vol. 10, no. 3, Institute of Development Studies, University of Sussex.

Wright, E.O. (1989) *The Debate on Classes*, Verso, London and New York.

Yeganeh, N. (1982) 'Women's Struggles in the Islamic Republic of Iran', in A. Tabari and N. Yeganeh, eds., *In the Shadow of Islam: The Women's Movement in Iran*, Zed Books, London.

Zabih, S. (1966) *The Communist Movement in Iran*, University of California Press, Berkeley and Los Angeles.

Zubaida, S. (1982) 'The Ideological Conditions for Khomeini's Doctrine of Government', *Economy and Society*, vol. 11, no. 2.

Newspapers, Journals and Periodicals

Ayandegan newspaper
Baseeje Khaharan newspaper
Enghelabe Eslami, newspaper
Ettellaat newspaper
Farzaneh women's magazine
Gosaresh
Hoghoughe Zanan
Iran Focus
Jebhe Ettellaat newspaper
Keyhan newspaper
Maiyar magazine
Payame Emrouz newspaper
Payame Hajar women's newspaper
Payame Zan women's magazine
Rouznameh Zan
Sobh newspaper
Zanan women's magazine
Zane Rouz women's magazine
Government Publications
The Constitution of the Islamic Republic of Iran
Iran Almanac and Book of Facts (Echo of Iran)
Iran Statistical Yearbooks, Islamic Republic of Iran, Plan and Budget Organisation
Statistical Centre of Iran, The Statistics For Large Industries, Iran
The Labour law

Primary Sources

80 interviews
348 questionnaires

Index

Index

181

CIA, *see* Central Intelligence Agency
class structure, 15–16, 21–3
    definition of, 23
    early, 29–31
    men's permission and, 113–14
co-educational schools, closure of, 67
Communist Unity, 130
compensation *Ojratolmesl*, 101
Constitutional Revolution (1906–11),
    32–3
contraception, increase in use of, 100

Dehghani, Ashraf, 57
Divar (Wall) (Farokhzad), 56
divorce, 54, 68, 109, 110
    reforms in, 100
Dokhtarane Iran (Iranian Women), 38
domestic domain, gendered roles in,
    111–13
domestic production, small-scale, 30
Doulatabadi, Seddighe, 39
dress, Islamic, *see* Islamic dress

Ebadi, Shirin, 101
Ebtekar, Masoomeh, 146
economy
    adaptation to capitalism, 97
    depression, 36
    growth, 45
    in 1990s, 94–6
    under Pahlavi, 35–60
    policies, reversal of, 94–121
    pre-revolution, 61–2
    pressures, 12, 14
    processes, 43–9
    see also employment
education
    female, 105
    gender segregation in, 70–73
    higher degrees, 106
    reform in, 103–8
employment, 9, 19, 20
    conforming and, 150
    at eve of revolution, 61–2
    gender segregation within, 89–92
    hierarchy of, 12, 13
    impact of Iran–Iraq war, 77–93
    Islamic sexual division in, 61–76
    in 1941, 37
    patriarchal relationships and,
        108–11

policies, reversal of, 94–121
return to, 12
unemployment, 64
urban, 48
women's place in, 5
see also economy
Enghelabe Farhangi Eslami (Islamic Cultural
    Revolution), 71–2
Entesharate Roshangaran
    (Enlighteners), 138
Ershade Eslami (Islamic Guidance), 73,
    81
Etehade Enghelabie Zanane Mobarez
    (Revolutionary Unity of Militant
    Women), 130
Etesami, Parvin, 39
Etezadi, Malekeh, 40
Ettehade Melli Zanan (National Union
    of Women), 130
Ettellaat (Information), 82
Ettellaat Banovan (Women's Information),
    42
European capitalist market, 29–31
extra-home activities, exclusion from,
    9, 70–73

Fallaci, Oriana, 50
family life, 79
    in Constitution of Islamic Republic
        of Iran, 66
    law reform, 98–103
    patriarchal relations in, 67–70
Family Protection Act (FPA) (1967), 51,
    68
Fanon, Frantz, 57
Farokhzad, Forough, 55–6
Farzaneh (Wisdom), 139, 140
Fatimah, as image, 11, 12, 64–5
Fedayeen Organisation, 133
female labour
    in private sector, 83–7
    in state sector, 77–82
    minimal demand for, 62–7
    in state ministries, 95
    see also economy; employment
feminists, secular/Muslim debate, 4–8
field research, 18–21
film industry, 138
Finnegan, R., 21
Firouz, Maryam, 41
First World War, 34

ministries, female workforce in, 95
power, centralisation of, 40
shifts in position in, 96–8
women's preference for work in, 87–9
status, socio-economic, 15–16, 21–3

tabaghe (social status), 23
Tabatabai, Etezadi, 6
Taleghani, Ayatollah, 57
Taleghani, Azam, 123–4, 136–7, 145, 147
Tashkilate Democratike Zanane Iran (Democratic Association of Iranian Women), 132
Tashkilateh Zanane Iran (Organisation of Iranian Women), 41
Tavaledi Digar (Another Birth) (Farokhzad), 56
teaching, 82
tobacco, boycott of, 32
trade union activities, 125, 126–9
Tudeh Party, 132

Union of Iranian Communists, 130
United States
embassy, 133
influence of, 49–50

velayat faqih (governance of the religious jurist), 58
Khomeini's theory of, 66
virginity, 110
test for, 55
vote, right to, 34, 42, 50

wages, 20–21
Walby, S., 14
White Revolution of the Shah and the People, 43, 50
WOI, *see* Women's Organisation of Iran
women publishers, 138
Women's Day celebration, declaration of, 67
women's journals/magazines, 139–42
flourishing of, 40–41
under state supervision, 42–3
women publishers and, 138
women's movement
rise of diverse, 32–4

women's newspapers, 139–42
flourishing of, 40–41
under state supervision, 42–3
women publishers and, 138
women's organisations, 40–41, 42–3, 146
flourishing of, 40–41
to support Islamic state, 132
under state supervision, 42–3
Women's Organisation of Iran (WOI), 51, 124
Rastakhiz party and, 52
women's publications
flourishing of, 40–41
under state supervision, 42–3
women publishers and, 138
women's responses, 15–18
early capitalist development, 29–31
individual, 148–9
to Islamic state, 130–38
reforms and, 31–5
to patriarchy, 122–55
Women's Society of Islamic Revolution, 124, 137, 145
Women's Solidarity Council, day of action, 132–3
working-class, 23
definition of, 25
working conditions, in industry, 126–9
World War I, 34

Yasan, Afsarmolok, 129
Yeganeh, N., 5

zakat (Islamic tax), 63
Zanan (Women), 120–21, 139, 140, 145
Zanan Dar Mobareze (Women in Struggle), 130
Zanane Iran (Women of Iran), 41, 42
Zanane Mobarez (Militant Women), 130
Zanane Pishraw (Progressive Women), 40
Zanane Tarafdare Nehzate Azadie Iran (Women's Adherents of Freedom Movement of Iran), 132
Zane Emruz (Today's Woman), 40
Zane Mobarez (Militant Woman), 40
Zane Rouz (Today's Woman), 69–70, 80, 139, 140, 1119
Zaynab, as image, 11–12, 64–5, 78